Unforgettable GALVESTON *Characters*

Unforgettable GALVESTON *Characters*

JAN JOHNSON

THE History PRESS

Published by The History Press
Charleston, SC
www.historypress.com

First published 2018

Manufactured in the United States

ISBN 9781467140232

Library of Congress Control Number: 2018942451

Notice: The information in this book is true and complete to the best of our knowledge. It is offered without guarantee on the part of the author or The History Press. The author and The History Press disclaim all liability in connection with the use of this book.

CONTENTS

FOREWORD

Jan Johnson has previously taken us on fascinating tours of Galveston Island, first "walking us" through its hallowed neighborhoods and then "driving us" to even further adventures across the entire Island. We learned who lived where and when (and who was buried where and when!), along with just how Galveston grew from a dangerous outpost to a bustling port to a polished jewel of a city. Behind all those Victorian homes, German churches and Wall Street–designed businesses, the men and women who staked their very souls and fortunes on the success and future of the Island stood their ground fearlessly. *Unforgettable Galveston Characters* beautifully introduces us to those Island pioneers (for better, for worse and those in between) who got here long before we did. From the businessmen to the bootleggers and musicians, the matrons and the myths, the bit players and the soaring stars who found international fame, Jan's book captures the personalities and determination of the men and women who ultimately set the tone and tenure of Galveston. Who knew that all those iron gates were placed there by such surviving spirits of steel?

Many Galvestonians proudly call themselves BOI, "Born on the Island." The "Unforgettable Characters" you'll meet in this book quite literally earned the original title of BOI—they "Built Our Island." They deserve to be known, honored and remembered, and Jan's words joyously do just that.

—Frank Billingsley,
Chief Meteorologist, KPRC Channel 2 News, Houston, Texas

PREFACE

Interspersed among the "few and far between" sites in *Beyond the Beaten Paths* (2012), my second guide introduced a few of the city's most notable residents, such as Edmund Reed Cheeseborough, the chief financier of the grade raising, 1938 pilot Douglas "Wrong Way" Corrigan and the 650 German POWs detained at Fort Crockett from 1943 to 1945.

Unforgettable Galveston Characters literally picks up where that book left off, profiling some of the Island's other intriguing and colorful personalities, many forgotten over the years. From wealthy to working class, famous or infamous, the Island's populace affected virtually every professional genre—from entertainment to sports, the medical industry, finance, politics and civics. This first book of Island characters primarily focuses on those from the world of entertainment (in its various forms), successful and inventive businessmen (and women) and community builders, with a few legendary personalities included for good balance (thus saving the fundamentalists, military men and sports celebrities for future sequels.)

Among the profiles in this book are twenty-one individuals, two families and five groups (including one of eighteen churchmen). While many lived on the Island most of their lives, the tales of other Galvestonians who gained fame off the Island, as well as those "undersung" heroes (and heroines), are also told.

"BOI" or "IBC"?

Basically, all Galvestonians—whether they stayed here or merely passed through—can be grouped according to how they arrived in the city. Either they were born here, the "BOIs" ("Born on the Island"), or they got here as quickly as they could, the "IBCs" ("Islanders by Choice"). Whether BOI or IBC, many of these residents most likely stood on the Galveston shore, digging their bare feet in the warm sand and wiggling their toes until their legs were fully submerged in its silky, fine silt, becoming engulfed by the mystique of Galveston Island and never wanting to leave.

Navigating This Book

For the most part, the six chapters of *Unforgettable Galveston Characters* are not strictly routed, as the first two guides were, simply because people tend to move around a lot sometimes—even *off* the Island. Instead, city addresses or locations are alluded to (when known) in many of the profiles, just in case the reader wants to view those homes and businesses still standing. For instance, the site of pirate Jean Lafitte's house, Maison Rouge, located on the south side of Harborside between Fourteenth and Fifteenth Streets, is noted even though the building is long gone. Now private property, the site is clearly marked by the State of Texas.

The one exception to this rule is the "Saints and Sinners" chapter, which moves from church to church going east to west. In short, the writer leaves it up to the readers on how to approach the subject of Galveston's unique characters—from one's own armchair is certainly acceptable.

As much as possible, documented facts are presented. In some cases, however, documentation was destroyed or simply disappeared, whether by accident or design. In that case, researchers must rely on personal memories and eyewitness accounts, which can be iffy at best. These and/or the interpretations of facts can be revised as new knowledge is uncovered over time.

However, please do be cautious of the term *legend*, or tales remembered in the oral tradition. Remember the games of "Gossip" or "Telephone" from your childhood? Just take them with a grain of salt. Instead, just enjoy these interesting, fun and sometimes astoundingly good stories about some of those truly unforgettable Galvestonians. Happy reading!

ACKNOWLEDGEMENTS

Since beginning this book in July 2016, I have had so much help and support from so many people, not only with their encouragement but also with suggestions for inclusions. My third book definitely generated a lot of interest, even before it was halfway completed.

First and foremost, a hearty and heartfelt debt of gratitude to my partner, Gene Bindhammer, for simply leaving me alone to write behind closed doors. Not only did he contend with a less than spotless house, but he even tended to the potty needs of my tuxedo kitty, Button, on several occasions—a real sacrifice for him. Also, to those who started me on this writing path, Sally and Jim Laney, who first suggested that I write historical guides to the city, thank you.

Additionally, I again want to acknowledge the late Tim Thompson, who recommended my mom, Dorris Stechmann Johnson, to serve as John Garner's secretary during the first year of his Historic American Buildings Survey, 1966–67. Her stories of that day's research around the dinner table generated my passion for Galveston's history.

To the other learned writers and researchers who came before, beginning the path I would eventually follow, I want to extend my gratitude to Jane Chapin and Carlotta Barker for their early work on the neighborhood guides and the annual *Galveston Historic Homes* brochures. Whether paid professionals, architectural scholars or passionate volunteers, they are all bonded by their intrinsic love for our Island city, its history and preservation through the written word. To this group, please add Kathleen Shanahan

Maca, who has come so far, so fast in her knowledge and reporting of many diverse subjects within the city's history.

As always, the staff of the Galveston/Texas History Center of the Rosenberg Library has been at my "beck and call" throughout my writing career. Even though their names change periodically, their dedication to its extensive collection has remained steadfast. First, there is former director, Casey Greene; now formally a "Rosenberg Library Scholar," he stays in the background, but he is still there. Sean McConnell promptly found my requested files, ephemera and information and held them aside at the ready for me. In his absence, Head of Special Collections Peggy Dillard and Kevin Kinney most capably filled in for him, as did, in the beginning of my research, Travis Bible. Also, many thanks for friend Scott Field, an experienced preservation architect who, unfortunately, never found a place on the Island.

Good friend and former student James Anderson not only shared his extensive collection of historic resource materials but was also ever ready to enlighten me through Find-a-Grave or with his own knowledge. In addition, James served as my computer guru during the book's finishing design phrase—so many computer skills to master in so little time!

I also want to acknowledge the members and presenters of the Jean Laffite Society for extending the depth of my knowledge and interest to that early era. To name a few: CPA Jeff Modzelewski, with his droll delivery, never ceases to amuse with his "Lafitte 101"; ever-ready Lou MacBeth especially for her research into Jewish pirates; and Michael and Diane Wonio, him for his hornpipe demonstration and his presentations about the lives of mariners and her for her research on ship's figureheads. I have also enjoyed having the ear of Donna Southern Resnicek, with whom I can compare notes.

Proving that as a teacher, she can be taught, I sincerely want to thank my Osher Lifelong Learning students, among them Ann Forrester for sharing her vivid memories and those of her husband, Harry, as well as "Tiny" Walker, Suzanne McClure and Retta Weber for sharing their family's stories of Galveston.

But mostly, I want to thank my friends Fran Card, proofreader Ruth Tobey and Charli Rohack for their continuous support and encouragement, but mostly for their friendship.

To the above-mentioned and many, many more…

"Thanks and Thanks and EVER Thanks!"
—William Shakespeare, *Twelfth Night*

INTRODUCTION

On her first trip to Texas, midwestern author Edna Ferber likened the city of Galveston to one of Charles Dickens's most haunting characters: Miss Havisham, the wealthy spinster left standing at the altar, frozen in time by her self-imposed isolation:

> *Here in Galveston the humidity was like a clammy hand held over your face. Yet the city had a ghostly charm. The scent of the tangled gardens hung heavy on the muggy air. The houses, pockmarked by the salt mist and the sun and heat and mildew, seemed built of ashes. Here was a remnant of haunted beauty—gray, shrouded, crumbling. What did they resemble? Of what did this city remind me? Miss Havisham, of course. That was it. Miss Havisham the spectral bride in* Great Expectations.

A character in its own right, the Island city has attracted likewise over the years, providing a haven for those who have to go somewhere else to escape where they were (whatever the reason), for its therapeutic vitamin "sea" or to escape their mundane lives in favor of their own private paradise—a "Fantasy Island" of sorts.

Perhaps its magnetic quality lies in its location: at the end of I-45, isolated in the Gulf of Mexico 2.5 miles from mainland America or its natural harbor and/or curvature. Whatever the reason, the surrounding sea served to both isolate those who live here as well as connect them, each to the other, as they share this slender sandbar.

Over the years, many have walked Galveston's shores, beaches, bays or bayous, leaving their footprints in the sand—only to be wiped clean by time and tide. However, the singular stories of the city's most captivating characters remain, simply too good to be forgotten. They are retold throughout the pages of this book.

FOUNDING FATHERS... AND MOTHERS

A Triumvirate of Visionaires

Historians credit Samuel May Williams, Thomas McKinney and Michel Menard with establishing the city in 1839, despite many twists and turns. Not without their faults, each followed his own individual path to the Island city during the state's beginnings to make his own unique contributions to its promise.

The elder statesman of the three was Samuel May Williams. Born in Providence, Rhode Island, on October 4, 1795, he was apprenticed at age fifteen to his commission merchant uncle, Nathaniel F. Williams, who taught his nephew the business of commerce at his shop on Bowly's Wharf in Baltimore.

After Argentina opened its port to Maryland's clipper ships in 1808, Samuel sailed as supercargo to its capital, Rio de la Plata, and became fluent in both Spanish and French. He also directly observed how a colony became a country, which would greatly benefit the Mexican colony turned Republic of Texas in the future.

Williams moved to the state from New Orleans in 1822, traveling with a young woman under the assumed name of Mr. and Mrs. E. Eccleston; it seems that he, like others, left the United States owing lots of money and

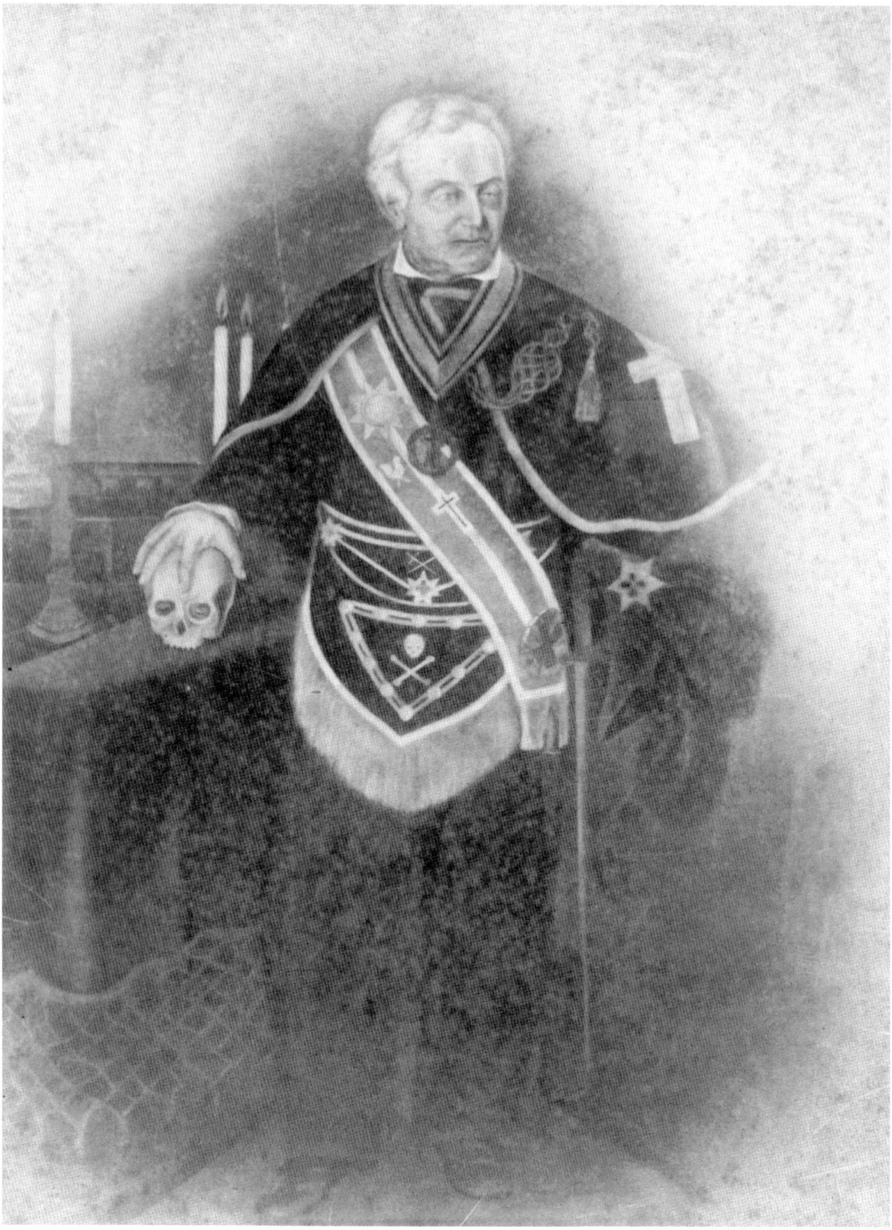

Samuel May Williams in Masonic attire. *Courtesy of the Rosenberg Library, Galveston, Texas.*

moved to an area with lax debtor laws. Keeping the child the woman bore him, he dumped "the Mrs." three years later in the hopes of marrying a younger woman.

Acquainted with Williams in New Orleans, Stephen F. Austin hired him in November 1823 as a translator and clerk, prompting the bookkeeper to drop his alias. Within three years, he had become his boss's surrogate—writing deeds, keeping detailed records and directing the colony's activities—while Austin was away from San Felipe. For these services, Williams was generously compensated with land.

Comfortable in his career, Samuel married Sarah Patterson Scott of Rhode Island in 1828. "Only coming home long enough to father the next child," he produced nine children. His wife was left by herself, raising the five who survived, as well as his son by "Mrs. E," according to a film shown during tours of his house at 3600 Avenue P in the past.

Partnering with Thomas F. McKinney, they opened a commission house at Quintana in 1833. "Home" to Sarah varied, as she divided her time between Galveston, Quintana and Velasco or spent time with her family on the San Jacinto River.

McKinney and Williams's new commission house succeeded in controlling the Brazos cotton trade for five years, earning the company a generous credit line with the United States. They used this to buy arms and supplies to help Texas win its independence from Mexico. Although McKinney was involved, Williams alone received the honorable title of "Financier of the Revolution," bestowed on him by author Ann Ruff in *Unsung Heroes of Texas.*

Part of those provisions included ships to prevent the Mexican army from getting men and supplies. They founded a second Texas Navy for the republic to protect the Gulf Coast from the enemy's blockade. Both partners moved to Galveston in 1838 to be closer to their fleet of seven ships before President Mirabeau B. Lamar sent the vessels to Yucatan.

The second president, Sam Houston, called the fleet back to Galveston, orders its commander did not receive. Learning of an impending naval invasion, Commodore Edwin Moore sailed back to defeat Mexico's warships on May 16, 1843. President Houston was not pleased, and Commodore Moore was court-martialed but acquitted. By 1845, 'the Texas Navy was no more," as Jim Bevil noted in an article for the *Houston Chronicle* on September 16, 2016.

Williams and McKinney then turned their focus—and money—to Menard's Galveston City Company. As part of the deal, they built a commission house on the wharf at 24th Street and Strand. Unfortunately, it was severely damaged during a hurricane in 1837.

McKinney left the partnership in 1842, so Sam Williams joined with his more successful brother, Henry Howell Williams of Baltimore, Maryland. While Sam concentrated on banking, H.H. bought the commission house and incorporated it into his own company.

Five years later, the Commercial and Agricultural Bank of Galveston was opened by Williams based on his 1835 charter, which had been approved by the republic the year Texas won its independence from Mexico. Although the bank had the right to print its own money, the timing came under a cloud of anti-banking sentiment in the state legislature. Attacking his C&A in the state courts for violating constitutional prohibitions, the legislators caused the Bank of Galveston to eventually fail, leading to the death of Samuel May Williams on September 13, 1858. The attending doctor noted that the Texas financier died of "no disease in particular but just a general debility—a giving way," according to biographer Margaret Henson. He was buried at the Episcopal Cemetery within the Broadway cemeteries by the Knights Templar, the chapter that Williams had founded on the Island.

THOMAS FREEMAN MCKINNEY WAS BORN on November 1, 1801, in Lincoln County, Kentucky. Twenty-three nomadic years later, the family settled in San Antonio, Texas. Refusing one of Austin's land grants on the Brazos River, Thomas chose to go to Nacogdoches to work at his uncle Stephen Prather's trading post. In 1827, he married Nancy Watts.

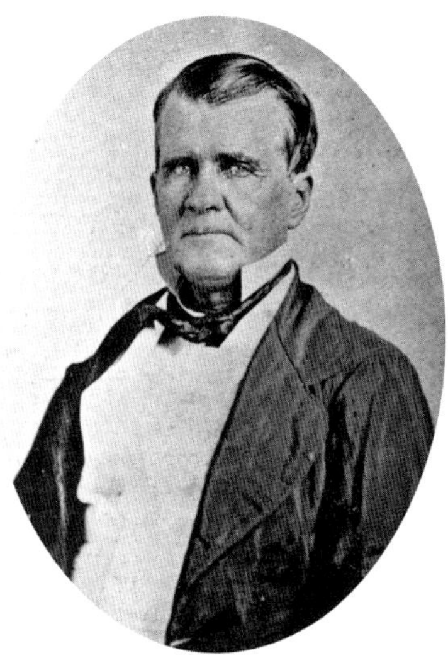

Thomas Freeman McKinney. *Courtesy of the Rosenberg Library, Galveston, Texas.*

While she ran their new store in Austin in 1830, McKinney partnered with Samuel May Williams, using his three steamships to transport cotton from their Quintana warehouse at the mouth of the Brazos River to New Orleans—a lucrative business arrangement for four years, such that they were able to invest in Michel Menard's Galveston City Company five years later.

Part of that deal was the construction of a warehouse and hotel on the Island. With Williams away on republic business, it was left to McKinney alone to supervise the construction of their warehouse at 24th and Strand. McKinney then built the Tremont Hotel at 23rd and Postoffice before turning his attention to the completion of two family homes, one for Williams and the other for himself, near 36th and Avenue P.

Simultaneously, during Texas's fight for independence from Mexico, McKinney secured a privateering license from Texas's provisional government that allowed him to legally attack Mexican ships in the Gulf that were preying on Texas-bound ships. As a result, he captured the *Correo de Mexico*. Using his own schooner, the *Liberty*, McKinney also supplied the Texas army. His obligations to Menard completed and extra money in his pocket, he split from the partnership, and his wife, in 1842.

Moving to Travis County, Thomas Freeman McKinney built an excellent stone house with an attached gristmill for his new Boston wife. With ranching and quarter horse racing as his new professions, he served in both the Texas House and Senate.

During the Civil War, he served as the Confederacy's special cotton agent. When the war ended, McKinney was illegally held liable for the South's debt. Being an honorable man, he paid it off, which eroded his once large estate to a mere $5,000. He died close to bankruptcy on October 2, 1873. More than one hundred years later, the site of his ranch and gristmill was named McKinney Falls State Park in 1976.

ALTHOUGH WILLIAMS AND MCKINNEY PLAYED large roles, the only man officially credited with founding the city of Galveston was Michel B. Menard. A French Canadian born fourteen miles north of Montreal in 1805, Menard started working as a fur packer for the Hudson's Bay Company at age fourteen, leaving five years later to join his two uncles in Kaskaskia, Illinois, in 1824. Following his Uncle Pierre, who had served as the state's Indian agent from 1813 to 1833, the illiterate Michel focused on Indian relations. Attending school for three months, he mastered the English language, setting out into the wilderness to complete his self-education with a book-filled backpack.

Along the way, he earned his living by rafting lumber—a most difficult and dangerous occupation—down the Illinois River to St. Louis and sometimes even on to New Orleans. Standing more than six feet tall with a powerful physique, he found himself running roughshod over a group of unpolished rowdies who tested their young boss. Not only did this build character,

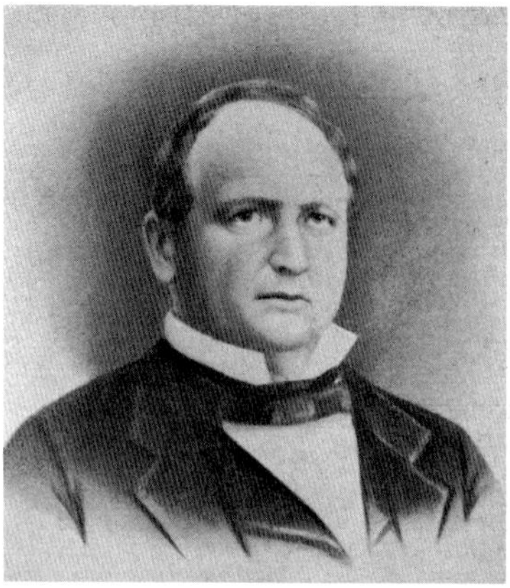

Michael B. Menard. *Courtesy of the Rosenberg Library, Galveston, Texas.*

but the experience also taught the young Menard managerial skills.

Observing his development, Pierre Menard was quite impressed with his nephew's shrewdness and ability to control such reckless individuals—qualities that identified him as an excellent Indian trader. Resembling Pierre in appearance, Michel also shared his respect for the Indians with similar drive and intentions, and this led to a job offer. Michel quickly accepted and became the only Indian trader in the territory of Arkansas among the Shawnees on the White River.

Mastering their language within a year, he quickly established himself, earning their trust and respect with his own sense of honor and integrity. With great affection, the tribe adopted him, making him one of their chiefs, a title he proudly held throughout his life.

From Shreveport, Louisiana, Michel moved in 1829 to Nacogdoches, Texas, where he built a large trading post and cultivated commerce with Native Americans there. Soon, he held a monopoly on that trade, even supplying the Indians with horses and mules. Within five years, he had accumulated forty thousand acres in the area. In partnership with Thomas F. McKinney, they built a sawmill and gristmill by the Trinity River to supply the needs of the new Texians on what is still known as Menard Creek.

As the Texas War for Independence approached around 1834, General Sam Houston engaged Menard, a Shawnee chief, to negotiate a peace treaty with the Delawares and Kickapoos. By doing this, Menard prevented all the Texas Indians from siding with Santa Anna.

At the same time, Menard, McKinney and Williams formed a new three-way partnership in the Galveston City Company to develop the East End of Galveston. Since non-Hispanics were not allowed to own property on the Island, this required a little financial finagling. Michel engaged Juan N. Seguin, a Mexican citizen, who obtained a headright at the location, which he then purchased from the Mexican citizen "on spec" in 1834.

Unfortunately, however, he was unable to start its development before the beginning of the war with Mexico, which forced the city's founder to pay the new republic another $50,000 in cash to clear his title. To secure the funds, Moseley Baker and John Kirby Allen (a future founder of Houston) were added to the company. Finally, on April 20, 1838, the sale of the first lots gave birth to the city, even though its official founding did not occur until the following year. The ownership of the Galveston Wharves, however, was not settled until 1869, with Menard's City Company having to give up one-third of its shares to the city.

On the personal side, Michel's life was as unsettled as his business dealings. His first wife had died of cholera on board a ship from New Orleans to Galveston in 1832. Four years later, he married his second cousin, Adeline of Kaskaskia, Illinois, but she died of yellow fever in July 1838. With the city's business dealings settling, its founder could finally turn his attention toward his personal life.

During this time, Augustus C. Allen had built a simple four-room house/office at 1605 33rd Street in the hopes of settling on the Island. However, he and his brother, John Kirby—both rough frontiersmen—were not accepted by the more refined Galvestonians and chose to move on to Houston. Three years later, Menard bought that house and enlarged it into a grand Greek Revival mansion on a ten-acre estate, just in time for his third wife, Mary Jane Riddle, to move in. Since he, as well as Williams, had experienced Mardi Gras while living in New Orleans, their housewarming reflected that theme.

Not long after, Tecumseh's brother paid a visit to the Shawnee chief to persuade him to return to the tribe with his family. The newly married Menard declined, however, because the new city's business responsibilities beckoned. Both men, however, enjoyed camping overnight in his spacious backyard—just like the old days.

When his third wife died in 1843, Michel married for a fourth and final time to a widow from Georgia named Rebecca Mary Bass. In 1850, he adopted her two daughters, Clara and Helen. Mrs. Menard gave birth to his only child, a son named Michael Doswell Menard, later that year—finally some stable happiness for Menard to celebrate.

On March 26, 1856, he and his wife hosted the first Mardi Gras party on Galveston Island, a grand Masque Ball. Despite the short notice, more than three hundred of the city's finest attended wearing splendid, expensive costumes and hiding behind various masks from all ages, from Hamlet to the pirate Lafitte, the Queen of the Gypsies, Silence, the printer Johannes Gutenberg, Dominican friars and even a few sailors. Their "disguises were so complete, it was impossible to recognize them." Unmasking later that evening revealed the city's elite "movers and shakers." Truly, it was a brilliant, novel affair given by an accomplished host and hostess, never to be surpassed for its beauty and splendor, as noted by all those who had "the pleasure of being present," according to the next day's *Galveston Tri-Weekly News*.

Consumed by his Republic of Texas, both as Congressman and financier, Michel Menard had invested in the house of Doswell, Hill & Company in 1847 but left its management to his partners. After several successful years, that business suddenly collapsed, leaving all its liabilities to him. Facing serious financial difficulties, he traveled the state to settle its affairs, overtaxing his once-robust health. Suffering intensely, he fell ill and died on September 22, 1856. A Catholic and a Mason, he was buried at the Catholic Cemetery within the Broadway cemeteries.

His obituary lauded his efforts to ensure the growth and prosperity of Galveston, noting his honesty, practicality and superb knowledge of men. An extensive reader, he displayed good business sense and excellent reasoning powers, and although he was impulsive, he was forgiving and appeasing. It ended with a suggestion that the City of Galveston should erect a monument to him, perhaps a statue on top of its courthouse. While that was never done, St. Patrick's Church did erect a 205-foot tower in his memory. Unfortunately, however, the 1900 Storm destroyed it.

As to each man's contribution, Samuel May Williams paved the way for the seaport city's U.S. credit line, while his partnership with McKinney resulted in ships, the vehicles of commerce. Thomas F. also constructed the first substantial buildings on the Island, including two residences. Risk-taking entrepreneur Michel Menard developed Galveston, laying the very foundations of the city, and invested in its economy. The most important element was how the talents of all three visionaries dovetailed at the right time and place to create the Queen City of the Gulf.

SURVIVING THE GREAT STORM: CLARA BARTON AND MAGNOLIA WILLIS SEALY

At the turn of the twentieth century, the city of Galveston, Texas, stood at the height of its prosperity and promise thanks to its natural harbor. The United States Congress had approved and appropriated funds to build a superport on Galveston Bay; construction was set to begin in September. Then, on the eighth of that month, this barrier island—located two miles off the coast—served its geological purpose. The city's once promising future sank beneath the very power from which it had prospered.

In one fifteen-hour period, 75 percent of the city's most populated part was swept clean by a seventeen-foot wall of water, inundating the Island from all sides—beach, port, East and West Ends. Current estimates place the death toll at ten thousand souls, but the exact number will never be known because its population was so transient. Many abandoned the stricken city, shrinking the population of thirty-seven thousand to about twenty thousand. Devastated but not destroyed, the survivors—men and women, rich and poor, black and white—pulled together to save themselves, their wealth and their lifestyles, capably lead by eight city fathers and one mother.

At 10:00 a.m. the following day, Mayor Walter C. Jones convened a group of prominent, successful businessmen to form the Central Relief Committee, each with his own very specific responsibility to avert further crisis. They declared that all able-bodied men had to work to earn their daily bread and presented it to all the other male survivors at 2:00 p.m. Quickly, they manned various committees—including finance, buildings, the hospital, correspondence and transportation—and went to work. Safety was ensured by armed guards patrolling the streets, with permission to shoot looters.

The gravest challenge facing the CRC was burial of the dead, both human and animal, so that the storm survivors would not become victims of an epidemic. Sharing that task were William A. McVitie, chairman of the relief committee, and Ben Levy, who would oversee all burials. While McVitie formed twelve different subcommittees at that 2:00 p.m. meeting to scour each of the twelve wards and gather the dead, Levy contemplated the magnitude of his job. All agreed that there was no time to properly identify each body, so he proposed a mass burial, which was immediately negated because the earth was too waterlogged.

By Monday, September 10, the CRC had decided on burial at sea. Because the storm's fury had ripped off their clothes, seven hundred bodies were placed in sacks and loaded on barges. To the horror of all, these dead washed back ashore overnight. The immediate solution: "Large funeral pyres were started on the beach...and the City was black with smoke, sickening the air with the odor of burning flesh," according to one eyewitness. Reluctantly, the men agreed that this would be the preferred method of disposal during the rest of the recovery, and the pyres burned constantly into the next year. When and wherever bodies were found, they were stacked with wooden debris and set aflame, with only personal eyewitnesses to chronicle the nameless victims in memoriam.

News of Galveston's great disaster reached Washington, D.C., and the president of the American Red Cross, Clara Barton, on September 10.

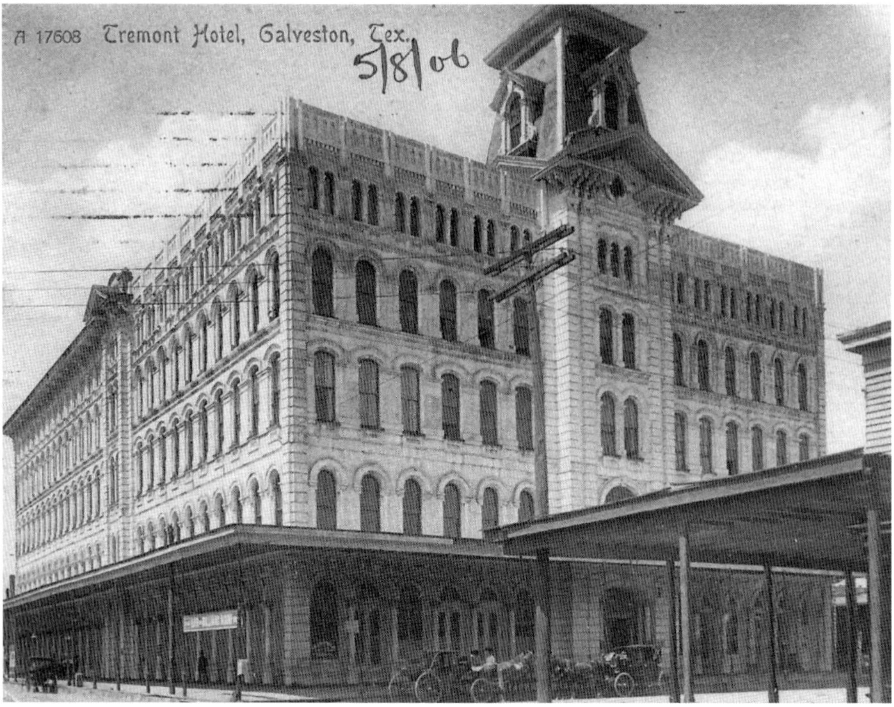

Tremont House, 23rd and Postoffice. *Author's collection.*

She arrived on the Island by train seven days later. The seventy-eight-year-old nurse became the ninth (and only female) member of the Central Relief Committee. Her nephew Stephen E. Barton, who would serve as general manager of the organization's operation, arrived one day later.

Although their headquarters was established on the Strand at 25th Street, Miss Barton chose to write and distribute pictorial press releases from her room at the Tremont House. Confirming the horrors of Galveston's tragedy to the world, she wrote, "[O]ne of those monstrosities of nature which defied exaggeration....The churches, the great business houses, the elegant residences of the cultured and opulent, the modest little homes of laborers...lay in splinters and debris piled twenty feet above the surface, and the crushed bodies, dead and dying, of nearly ten thousand of its citizens lay under them."

Thankfully, the world responded most generously. The first two weeks brought emergency relief for sanitation and public health. Miss Barton's regular reports to the headquarters in Washington, D.C., emphasized the

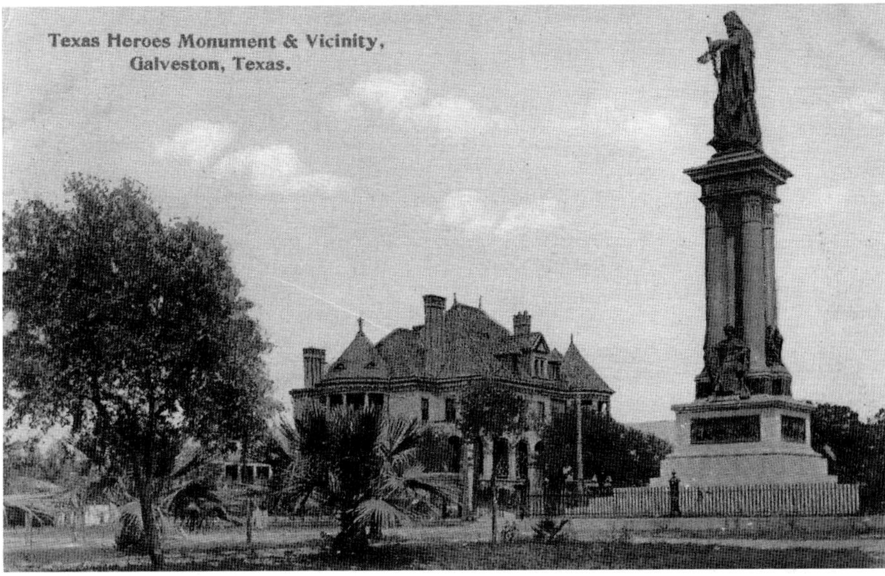

George Sealy Mansion, Open Gates behind Texas Heroes Monument. *Author's collection.*

necessities of survival—food, clothing, cash donations and disinfectants. Furniture, building supplies and linens followed. Thanks to Miss Barton's pleas, trainloads of relief supplies rolled into Galveston through January 1901.

Inspired by her presence and persistence, twenty-six Galveston women formed the Red Cross Auxiliary No. 1 to "help Miss Barton with her work." One of them was the matriarch of the Sealy family of the Open Gates at 25th and Broadway, Mrs. Magnolia Willis Sealy. Although not born on the Island, she acted from "her devotion [to] her beloved Galveston Island."

A leader among ladies, Sealy served as one of twelve chairwomen supervising the distribution of relief supplies in each of the twelve wards. She recruited the other women in her household, all of whom worked seven days a week, from 8:00 a.m. to 6:00 p.m. In a letter dated September 24, her daughter Ella described the experience to her absent sister, Margaret: "What Work! What work we have done and what work there is still to be done!! We...roll up our sleeves and...sort through boxes of clothes...to deliver to the wards." She continued, "The other day we heard a boy whistle on the street as he walked along and we all stopped...it was the first joyous sound we had heard; anything gay or bright in dress, or manner, seems utterly out of place."

By the end of the month, the immediate crisis had been averted, and Magnolia Sealy found time to host a fundraiser during an informal afternoon reception to honor Miss Barton, seeking other volunteers. In all, 150 Galveston women volunteered during the recovery. Speaking very deliberately but beautifully, the aged Red Cross president commended their work: "The best ladies of the city are heart and hand…canvassing the town through all its wards to see personally after the needs of the sufferers."

But Mrs. Sealy's work had just begun, as the matriarch took a leading role in the foundation of the Women's Health Protective Association (later known as the Galveston Civic League), modeled on similar organizations in New York and Philadelphia. On March 5, 1901, sixty-six prominent women, each from her own previous faith-based philanthropic endeavors, dedicated their own persistence, experience and talents to make the Island cleaner, healthier and more beautiful. Sealy was named to its first executive committee.

Its first and primary task was the beautification of the city. With her gardening knowledge and collection of tropical plants, she took a leading role in re-landscaping the city as the men's grade raising project progressed. After much studious research and investment, they chose stately live oaks, towering palms and a bushy shrub from Jamaica, the exotic and fragrant oleander, to decorate the Island city. Through their initial efforts under Mrs. Sealy's leadership, Galveston grew to become the "Oleander City." When the Central Relief Committee moved back into commerce in February 1901, the WHPA/GCL took over burial responsibilities because unclaimed skeletons were unearthed in odd places as late as 1908.

Simultaneously with her civic duties, Mrs. Sealy was arranging memorials for her beloved husband, George, who passed away on December 14, 1901. She commissioned Louis Comfort Tiffany to design a stained-glass window, entitled "Jesus Blesses the Little Children." Nicholas Clayton was engaged to enlarge the alcove and installed it in 1906. It still hangs above the altar at Trinity Episcopal Church today. In the Broadway cemetery, she turned to the New York architectural firm of her home, McKim, Mead & White, which designed an obelisk to mark the graves of the Sealy family. That mission completed, she turned her attention toward the African American community, helping to form the Colored Relief Society in 1909.

Magnolia Willis Sealy's activities in the social and civic life of Galveston only ended when she died on November 8, 1933. Her accomplishments and memory lived on through her seven children and one nephew, John Sealy Jr., who named his oil company the Magnolia Petroleum Company after his favorite aunt.

THE KEMPNERS

Throughout its history, Galveston, Texas, has had a large number of prominent Founding Fathers. While many were active during limited years, others continued to contribute to the city's culture, progress and prosperity over generations. The Kempners, a Jewish business family who never forgot their humble beginnings, were one of the latter. With the solid foundation of entrepreneurial successes laid by its patriarch and his eldest son, future generations continue to serve their civic responsibilities, catering to both humanitarian and artistic causes.

The founder of the family was Herschel Kempner, born in Russian Poland on March 7, 1837. The city of his birth was Krzapice, a real-life "Fiddler on the Roof" village. To escape service in the czar's army, he immigrated to America in 1854. In New York City, he changed his given name to Harris and worked primarily as a bricklayer, studying English at night.

He moved to Cold Springs, Texas, in Jacinto County four years later, where he was an itinerant peddler. When the Civil War began, Harris fought for the Confederacy. An injury led to his promotion to quartermaster sergeant, an ideal position for a future shopkeeper.

He found his way to the bustling port city of Galveston in 1870. In partnership with Marx Marx, they opened a wholesale grocery store that grew to the largest in the state, perhaps even in the South. Now a prosperous entrepreneur, Harris met Eliza Seinsheimer on a business trip in 1871. Known as "Lyde," she was a member of a prominent German Jewish family from Cincinnati, Ohio. Immediately smitten by her youth and vivaciousness, he courted her, proposed and married her on March 6, 1872. Indulging his new wife, they moved back to her hometown for the birth of their firstborn son, Isaac "Ike" Herbert Kempner, on January 14, 1873. They returned to Galveston, where they raised a balanced family of eight, four girls and four boys, in their spacious home at 20th Street and Avenue M.

In 1885, Harris lost his investment in the Island City Savings Bank. After he reinvested, he persuaded other local businessmen to keep it solvent by doing the same. Elected president of the reorganization committee, the Kempner patriarch reformed its business practices, saving the financial institution. The following year, he dissolved his partnership with Marx to turn his full attention to the state banking industry by buying stock in national banks of nine small Texas cities.

To further cement the family's fortunes, Kempner focused on the transportation of cotton. He bought shares in the Gulf, Colorado and Santa

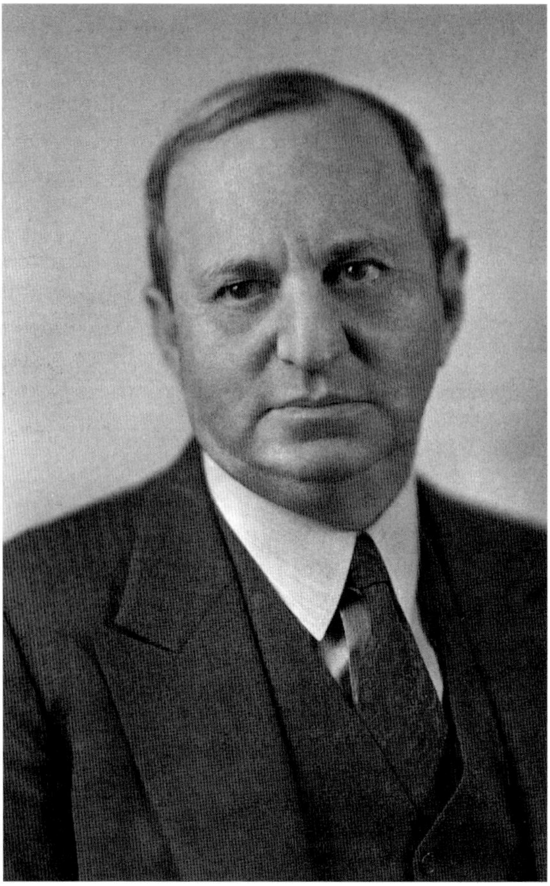

Isaac "Ike" H. Kempner. *Courtesy of the Rosenberg Library, Galveston, Texas.*

Fe Railroad, becoming a lifelong member of that company. At the beginning of the Gay Nineties, he was appointed to the Galveston Deep-Water Committee, a body that planned to expand the port along west Galveston Bay; however, his unexpected death on April 13, 1894, ended that.

In Virginia at Washington and Lee University, Ike was immediately called home to take over the family enterprises. Over the years, he would greatly diversify their holdings, but those plans were put on hold by the 1900 Storm. In the immediacy of the disaster's aftermath, Kempner's eldest son originated the Commission form of government to avert further disaster. Years later, in a speech he delivered to the Galveston Historical Society on February 12, 1946, I.H. recognized it as "an efficient weapon" and method of administration to "deal with the physical & fiscal problems arising from havoc & destruction wrought by wind & waves," which gave rise to the

"Galveston Spirit," with a warning originally issued by Teddy Roosevelt in 1906 never to forget that "the root of the matter lies in the character of the individual citizen." Those serving as commissioners are human and, as such, subject to dishonesty and incompetency.

After the Great Storm, Governor Joseph D. Sayers appointed five to the Central Relief Committee—the best of the Island's citizenry, men with "the sincerity of their service in the mission...of economic and civic rescue." Each was charged with his own responsibility according to his strengths. Kempner was appointed as finance commissioner of CRC in 1901. His initial task was to work with the others to marshal assets to fund "protective & progressive municipal improvements" (e.g., the seawall and grade raising). Although he officially retired from government work in 1915, he was drafted for mayor from 1917 to 1919.

Simultaneously, Kempner expanded the family's business interests to include a cotton warehouse, serving on the Galveston Cotton Exchange board in various capacities for more than fifty years. He then moved on to real estate speculation (both on and off the Island), which was shortly followed by an investment in a sugar refinery.

In 1908, I.H. Kempner partnered with W.T. Eldridge in a small sugar refinery along the Brazos River west of Houston. Renaming it the Imperial Sugar Refinery, he asked his brother Dan to serve as president, with Eldridge as general manager. When its workers needed houses to live in, the "company town" of Sugar Land evolved around it. While it grew, the Kempners spearheaded the building of the Hotel Galvez in 1911 to symbolize the city's return as a tourist destination.

When state insurance laws changed, the poorly capitalized American National Insurance Company (ANICO) in Houston became available. Marching into Ike's office in 1904, W.L. Moody convinced Kempner to partner with him in the venture and move the company to Galveston.

Two years later, while Ike was out of town—perhaps attending to his new sugar refinery—a member of the state insurance board, Tom Love, visited with Moody and suggested that more capital was needed in the new and growing ANICO. When he returned, Moody met with Kempner but told Ike that Love had insisted that one family sell out to the other. Of sterling integrity and harboring "a noble but naïve belief in decency of others," Ike did just that, according to Gary Cartwright's book *Galveston: A History of the Island.*

Two years after the transaction, in an impromptu encounter, Love confessed his surprise that he had sold out, prompting Ike to recount his meeting with Moody to the now secretary of the U.S. Treasury. After Love revealed the truth, the honorable Kempner realized that Moody had simply lied to him. Admitting his own gullibility, he chronicled the incident in his memoirs: a "typical instance where an associate's cupidity and duplicity triumphed over my own stupidity." That same year, the Kempners founded First Texas Prudential Life, headed by younger brother Stanley. However, the rift between the two families still persists today.

After a long, productive and respected life, Isaac Herbert Kempner passed away Monday, August 1, 1967, at his Broadway home after short a illness. His public funeral service was held the following Wednesday morning at Temple B'nai Israel, his family requesting that mourners make charitable contributions as memorials. Noting his many business successes, the *Galveston Daily News* lauded Ike Kempner as a "leading figure in finance, industry, philanthropy & government."

With his passing, the Kempner legacy passed to his son, Harris Leon, who had married a lifelong friend, Ruth Levy, in 1939. A BOI herself—born on November 26, 1917, to Marion J. and Alma L. Levy—she graduated from the University of Texas–Austin in 1937 with a major in history and a minor in government during a time when most women didn't consider college. Cut from a different cloth, Ruth acknowledged herself as a housewife but added "troublemaker" to her self-description.

Ruth served as head of the Red Cross disaster relief committee. During the Texas City explosion in 1947, she was at the scene when the second ship, the *Grandchamp*, exploded. Rescuing a little boy, the two immediately started toward her Island home, hiding in a ditch when the *High Flyer* blew up. For several hours, her husband thought that she'd been killed, until she appeared at the front door, ward in hand.

During World War II, Ruth joined the League of Women Voters. What followed during the next decade were heated discussions at the dinner table regarding her father-in-law's Commission form of government. Ruth argued that it had become inefficient, corrupt and partisan, citing the number of illegal activities that flourished in the city (e.g., Maceo's gambling empire and the Postoffice trade) as proof. In 1960, the troublemaker in her mounted a campaign to replace it with the Council-Manager form.

Securing a place on the Citizens Charter Committee, Ruth helped draft a new charter outlining the change. Eight city council candidates supported it, and six were elected that year, including Ruth herself—the first female councilman—to serve under Mayor Edward Schreiber. From 1961 to 1963, neither form of city government was discussed in the family home. However,

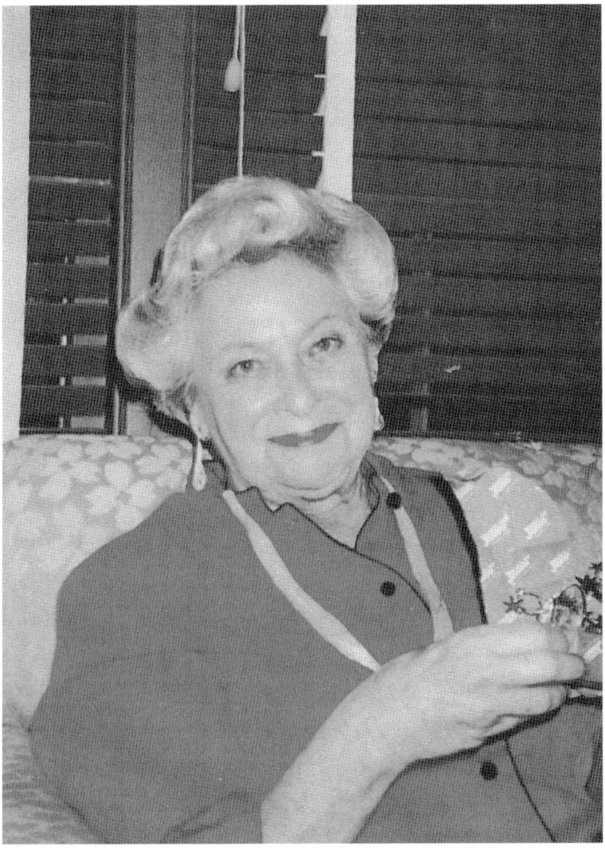

Left: Ruth Levy Kempner. *Courtesy of the Kempner family.*

Below: Texas City disaster, April 16, 1947 site map.

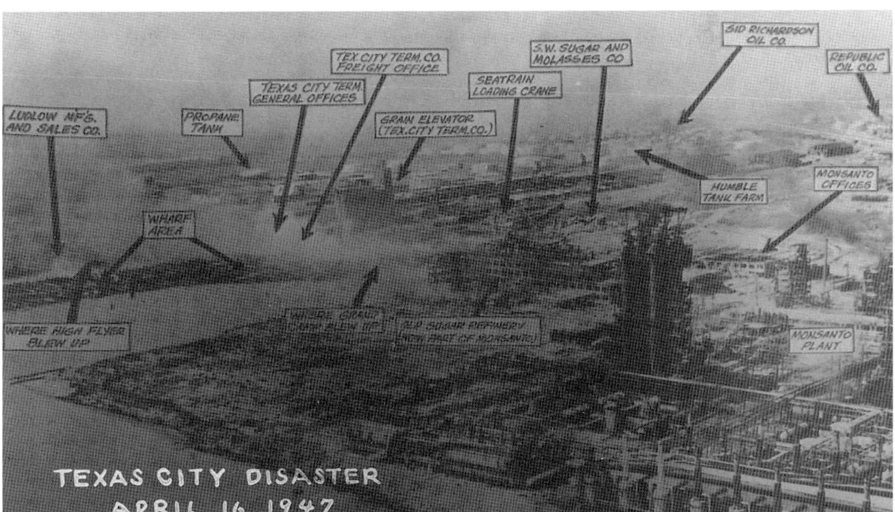

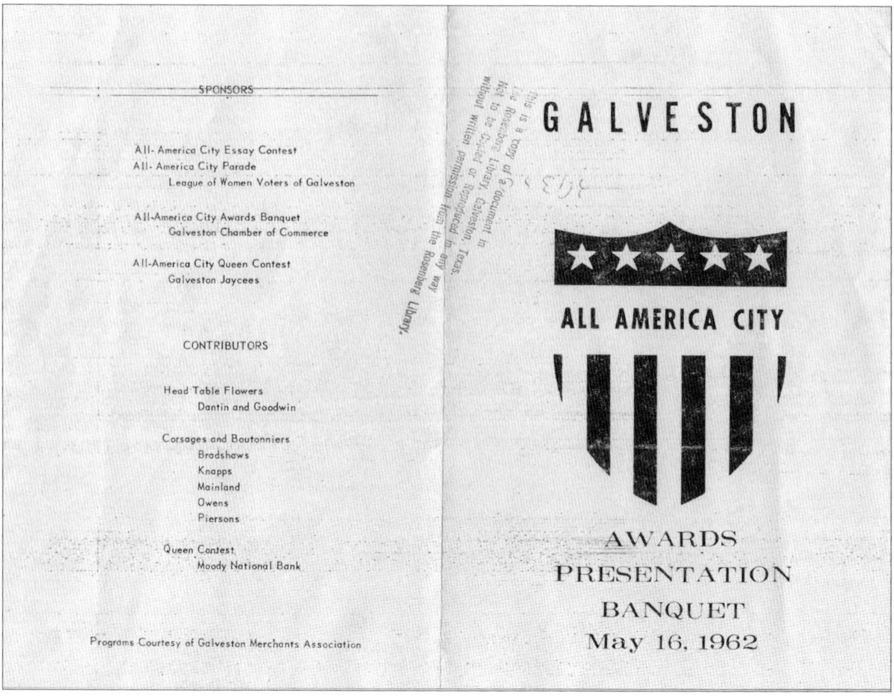

SPONSORS

All-America City Essay Contest
All-America City Parade
League of Women Voters of Galveston

All-America City Awards Banquet
Galveston Chamber of Commerce

All-America City Queen Contest
Galveston Jaycees

CONTRIBUTORS

Head Table Flowers
Dantin and Goodwin

Corsages and Boutonniers
Bradshaws
Knapps
Mainland
Owens
Piersons

Queen Contest
Moody National Bank

Programs Courtesy of Galveston Merchants Association

GALVESTON

ALL AMERICA CITY

AWARDS
PRESENTATION
BANQUET
May 16, 1962

"All America City," banquet program. *Courtesy of the Rosenberg Library, Galveston, Texas.*

after it was implemented, the Council-Manager form proved successful after Hurricane Carla in September 1961, as the city recovered quickly with minimum loss of life.

To honor the transition, Galveston was named an "All America City," one of eleven such U.S. cities in 1962. The project was sponsored by National Municipal League and *Look* magazine. The weeklong celebration, May 13–18, was highlighted by the Galveston All America City Awards Presentation Banquet, held that Wednesday at the Moody Center. That event was sponsored by the chamber of commerce, which sold tickets for five dollars per person. Charles B. Smith, chamber president, served as master of ceremonies, while Lockwood B. Seegar, *Look* magazine's regional representative, and Edward C. Sullivan, representing the National Municipal League, bestowed the honor on Mayor Edward Schreiber.

Island business and the Kempner interests continued to progress over the next twenty-five years. Three years later, Imperial Sugar bought out Holly Sugar, making it the second-largest American refinery. However, Harris

Kempner Sr. wouldn't see that, as he died unexpectedly on the tennis court in September 1987.

Similar to his grandfather I.H., "Shrub" Kempner was called on to take over the family finances. With degrees from both Harvard and Stanford in 1969, he started making "remarkably good" investments for H. Kempner Company. Secure in his new position, in 1982 Shrub opened his own investment company, Kempner Capital Management. With his father's company his primary client, Shrub soon worked his own Kempneresque financial magic. One writer even dubbed the junior H.L. the "Wizard of Galveston," thus fulfilling his father's prophecies, according to Harold M. Hyman, from 1981 and 1963, respectively, that the family does "better in succeeding generations" "by working for the group and not self alone."

ISLAND ENTREPRENEURS

Dramatic Women

By the early 1920s, Galveston Island had recovered from the devastation of the 1900 Storm. As the building of the seawall and grade raising progressed, prominent women turned their thoughts away from the replanting of the city toward more intellectual pursuits. While most of their social clubs centered on church and children, several literary study groups formed, the oldest of which was the Wednesday Club, with its focus on modern dramatic literature.

On February 16, 1922, it sponsored an exclusive soiree at the W.L. Moody home at 27th and Broadway. With three hundred prominent citizens in attendance, the director of the New Orleans Little Theatre, Oliver Hinsdell, read Eugene O'Neill's 1920 Pulitzer Prize–winning play, *Beyond the Horizon*. This event proved to be the inciting incident toward the establishment of a Little Theatre on Galveston Island.

One year later, a group of ten ladies formed the nucleus of the Little Theatre Board of Directors. At the request of Mrs. P.A. Drouilhet, they invited Peter Ames Vincent of New York to speak about the Little Theatre's role in the future of American drama and playwrights. Mrs. Herman Nussbaum urged all members to become patronesses of the performing arts by donating just $5 each. With a bank balance of $330, this meeting was declared a successful launch of a Little Theatre on Galveston Island.

They hired Vincent to direct a trial production on June 1 at the Garten Verein in Kempner Park. He chose *The Truth*, a difficult four-act comedy written by American playwright Clyde Fitch. The opening night audience filled the pavilion to capacity, and receipts exceeded expenditures, increasing the number of patrons to 126. Vincent was hired as artistic director, adopting the title "Regisseur."

Three seasons later, the company came of age, both artistically and financially. The fifth play of that season was Henrik Ibsen's classic story *A Doll's House*, its first production in America that year. As soon as the curtain opened on April 15, 1926, Vincent's set of the kind of home "a doll-wife would keep" garnered the capacity crowd's applause. Local theater critic Howard Stanley Aronson noted that the play was "the first shot fired in the war for woman's intellectual independence."

Lead by board president Mrs. I.H. Kempner, the theater's executive committee honored all of Galveston's actors with a benefit banquet at Gaido's on Murdock's Pier, 23rd and Seawall, on May 24. The climax of the evening was Vincent's parody of *A Doll's House*, with the cross-dressed cast set as a typical Little Theatre rehearsal: Miss Thompson as the director and Vincent as Nora. Renamed *A Doll's Souse*, the program stated that it was "Done Under Pressure in the interest of neither Science, Morals, nor Education." This banquet and burlesque provided the pin money for a proposed new playhouse.

From 1923, the plays were staged at various locations. However, the women of the board wanted a home of their own for their Little Theatre. This became a reality during the summer of 1926. A building on the southwest corner of 18th and Postoffice Streets was renovated into a modern theater, seating 238 patrons. Boasted to be "one of the most modern theatrical plants in the State of Texas," the new theater debuted at the first play of the 1926–27 season.

This acquisition brought the Little Theatre of Galveston into the legality of the business realm. As such, the ladies had to bow to their men to carry out the business roles. Chartered by the State of Texas, this new organization was born on June 8, 1926, with its stated mission being "to support and maintain a literary undertaking…for drama of all ages." The three men who "voluntarily associated" themselves in the formation of this private nonprofit organization were W.L. Moody Jr., George Sealy and I.H. Kempner, a triumvirate of the Island's wealthiest and most influential families—quite possibly the only time they were ever associated together.

The little playhouse thrived until its Regisseur fell ill in 1928. Even though he continued to direct from his hospital bed through his surrogate, Gladys Ann Kirschner, it soon became apparent that he was critically ill and would not recover. Peter Ames Vincent died on April 16, 1930, signaling the beginning of the end for the Little Theatre of Galveston.

However, the dramatic women had produced a theater that paid its own way through its work in stagecraft for twelve years. In addition, they created a community of players within the Island community that represented the economic, social and cultural diversity of Galveston, producing a democratic organization—truly, a theater of the people.

In 1946, the spotlight again illuminated the stage at 18th and Postoffice with a new generation of players. In honor of its twenty-fifth anniversary in 1948, the theater staged a world premiere of the drama *Front Porch*, written by an obscure midwestern English professor, William Inge. His first of many, the play opened on Broadway as *Picnic* in 1953.

The *Silver Anniversary Program* listed the 1,042 actors and actresses who "tread the boards" of Galveston's Little Theatre from 1923 to 1948 in its repertory of eighty-nine plays. Of these "dramatis personae," Natalie Moskowutz wrote, "Those 1,042 Galvestonians are, we feel, the best testimony to the vigor of this community theatre. May future members be as proud as we are to add their names to this list."

Among them was a young lady named Katherine Helmond, but her friends called her Patsy. Raised by both mother and grandmother in a devout Catholic home, she attended Ursuline Academy, where she performed in many pageants and plays. Before her graduation from Ball High School in 1948, she volunteered at the local theater—painting scenery, cleaning the building and pulling the curtain. Only once did her name appear as part of the cast: in December 1950, when she played Sister Joanna of the Cross in *Cradle Song*.

As early as 1955, Patsy landed her first leading role in a full-length film as reported by the *Galveston Daily News*. While attending Bob Jones University, she portrayed Irene of Cyrus in *Wine of Morning*, about "Barabbes." The article also noted that she was the daughter of Thelma Malone at 3906 Avenue O.

From there, she moved on to the Houston Playhouse, then the Margo Jones Theater in Dallas and, finally, New York from the 1950s to the 1960s, where she debuted in the Catskills summer stock in *As You Like It*. To make ends meet, Patsy taught acting classes and managed a playhouse in upstate New York for three seasons before moving to Broadway, where she eventually earned a Tony nomination for Eugene O'Neill's *The Great God Brown* in 1973.

Movie roles followed for this character actress in *The Hindenburg*, *Family Plot* and *Overboard*, but Ms. Helmond gained the most fame through television. She made numerous guest appearances, from *Gunsmoke* to *The Bob Newhart Show*, and received rave reviews for the roles of Emily Dickinson in *Meeting of Minds* and Hedda Hopper in *Liz: The Elizabeth Taylor Story*.

She honed her comedic skills through the American Film Institute, which led to her two most popular TV roles. The first was the ditzy matriarch Jessica Tate on ABC's *Soap*, which ran from 1977 to 1981. Nominated for an Emmy three out of the four years it ran, Ms. Helmond won a Golden Globe for that character in 1980. She would reprise Jessica in two other sitcoms, *Benson* and *Everyone Loves Raymond*.

She is best remembered, however, as the free-spirited Mona Robinson on *Who's the Boss*, which ran from 1984 to 1992. This feisty, liberated grandmother earned Ms. Helmond two Emmy nominations and a Golden Globe in 1989. Most recently, she voiced the Model T known as "Lizzie" in all the *Cars* movies (2008, 2011, 2012 and will again in the next one).

Former Galvestonian Katherine "Patsy" Helmond has successfully spent four decades on stage and screen, following her passion that, as the character actress herself, was also "Born on the Island."

THE REYMERSHOFFERS: A LEGACY OF ISLAND BUSINESSMEN

Jan Reymershoffer, born in 1808 at Holleschau Mahren, Austria, achieved great business success that resulted in his election to the Reichstag at Vienna. With political unrest in Bohemia, he moved his family of six to the United States, arriving in Galveston in December 1854 aboard the ship *Ammerland*. He brought with him enough goods to stock a small mercantile store, where he would teach his sons, John Jr. and Gustav, the business.

While working for their father, the ambitious sons opened their own general commission house, specializing in imported glass and porcelain ware. They also listed the old Galveston Cracker Factory among their interests, and the elder, John Jr., served as director of the First National Bank. Unfortunately, their father died on October 10, 1876, two years before they achieved their greatest business success.

The brothers moved their offices to the Duhamel Building, 2202–10 Mechanic, the following year. Here, John penned an unfinished note outlining a "new process" of milling flour by "reducing grain by two or more distinct grindings," which led to their next business venture.

In 1878, they invested $50,000 in the Texas Star Flour Mill, located on the north side of Avenue A (now Harborside Drive) between 20th and 21st Streets. When it was opened to the public on July 6 the following year, it was hailed as the leading plant of its kind. Large additions were made over the next ten years—a grain elevator, a rice mill and a railroad—as they cultivated new business with the West Indies, Mexico and Central America. Company profits soared to $500,000 as the mill became the largest individual success story of Galveston's first industrial era.

To protect his thriving business, the elder Reymershoffer applied for official recognition from the U.S. Department of the Interior. The Texas Star Flour Mills received written declaration no. 30,060 on June 8, 1897, from the United States of America Patent Office, granting "J. Reymershoffer, an officer of said corporation" full rights "of a certain trademark…for Flour, Rice, Meal and Grits." Included with it were samples of original flour bags, with their distinct logos.

As their business thrived, the brothers could well afford to build their respective dream homes in 1886. On property that their father had purchased twenty years earlier, between 13th and 14th Streets on Postoffice, John's large house stood in the middle of the block. Featuring a tower room, a balcony and a conservatory, it became the Phi Chi medical fraternity with eighteen apartments in 1925; unfortunately, it was demolished in December 1956.

Gus's house stood on the northwest corner of 13th Street. Along with the checkered gray-and-red cement sidewalk so fashionable in the late 1880s, its original cast-iron front gate still bears the name "G. Reymershoffer." Within the home, its interior woodwork, tiling and sheaves of wheat etched into the glass of the front door are original, and a stained-glass Texas Star logo hangs in the stairwell.

Their mother, Mrs. Clara Reymershoffer, owned both 509 13th Street and 1305 Postoffice, built 1891 and 1894, respectively, across the street; only the latter is still standing. Although they were of Austrian birth, Galvestonians considered the family German because many of their neighbors were members of an elite German social club.

Profits were strong in 1898, when the directors met in a called meeting on March 24. John Jr. was listed as president and his brother Gus vice-president. A third generation, John's son, was listed as secretary/treasurer; his minutes, handwritten with a turn-of-the-twentieth-century flourish, called for a 5 percent dividend to all partners.

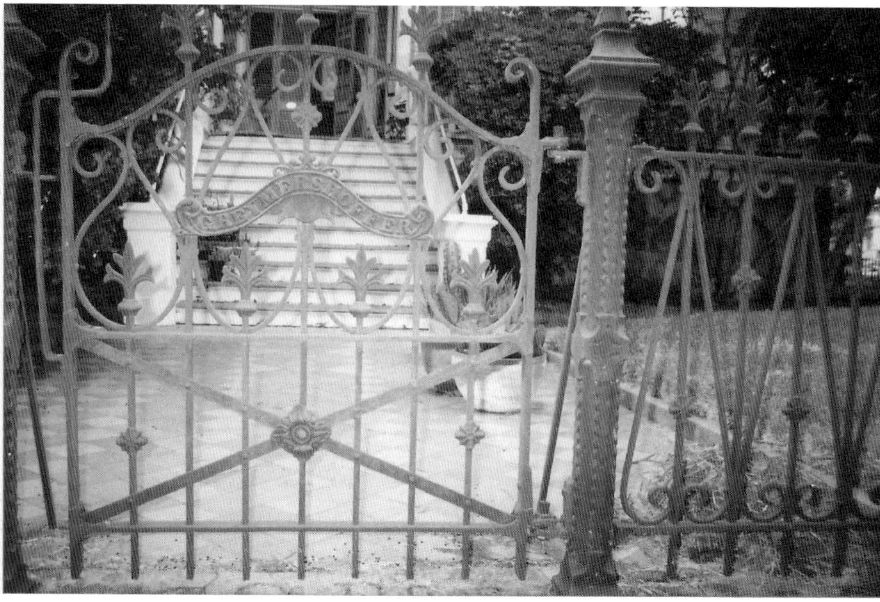

Photograph of Gus Reymerhoffer's front gate, 13th and Postoffice. *Author's collection.*

It was not "all work and no play" for the Reymershoffers. Family papers included various invitations—from "Ladies Day" at the Galveston Artillery Club to an invitation to a wedding in St. Louis. They were involved with the national Mercantile Club and exchanged Christmas greetings with many national food companies, including the H.J. Heinz Company of Pittsburgh. The families traveled frequently during the 1890s, chronicling their trips in photographs. One photograph showed Gus with his wife and three daughters—Elsa, Gertrude and Hilda—at Niagara Falls, New York.

John Jr. collapsed on a Broadway sidewalk and died suddenly on December 12, 1899, while visiting his two daughters in New York City. An autopsy revealed that the cause was apoplexy, "a result of mental strain." The *Galveston Daily News* remembered him as "one of the most prominent and enterprising citizens," with "sterling integrity and quiet, unassuming way." At the time of his death, he was the Austrian consul at Galveston and had served one term as city alderman. Flags were flown at half-staff in honor of "this loyal American citizen…of foreign parentage and birth." His survivors were his wife, Beda, and five children: John III, Max, Charles, Anita and Thea.

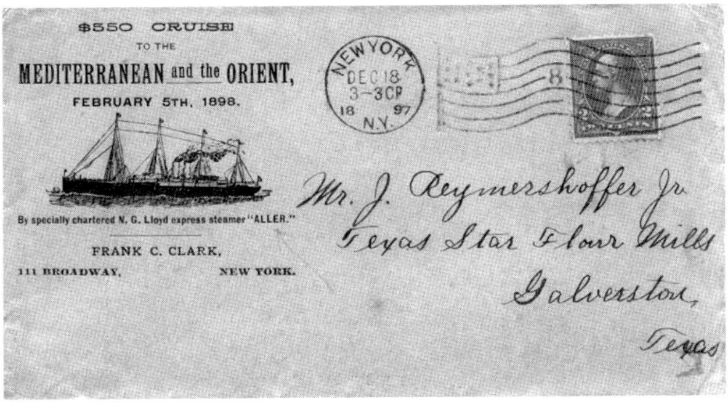

Envelope addressed to Mr. J. Reymershoffer Jr., postmarked December 18, 1897, from New York aboard N.G. Lloyd Steamer *Aller*.

Business continued as usual at the Flour and Rice Mills until "the storm and holocost [*sic*] of September 8, 1900," according to a handwritten note. One of the storm victims was the widow Clara, whose death was recorded in a list of bodies found on October 23.

In minutes dated May 17, 1902, President John III detailed the damages sustained by the mill and noted the difficulty in making repairs, ending his speech with, "[T]he entire plant [is] fully restored in better shape than ever before." He also noted the importance of "the discovery of crude petroleum near Beaumont [Spindletop] in January 1901" as a better and cheaper fuel source. The majority shareholder was noted as his mother, Beda; Uncle Gus was vice-president and the absent Charles was secretary.

In failing health for some time, Gustav Reymershoffer passed away peacefully on November 18, 1903, with his sister, Ottille Jordon, at his side. His wife, Eugenia, was in Milwaukee with their three daughters. The *Galveston Daily News* remembered him as "one of the prime movers to establish… trade with the West Indies." His widow died in 1961 at age ninety-eight. Descendants of the family lived in the house until it was sold in 1985, after the death of his daughter, Elsa.

The Reymershoffers sold their interests in Texas Star Flour Mill to M. Edward Lasker and associates of Galveston in 1904. Thirty years later, the business was sold again to Burrus and Kell from Dallas, who ran the mill until 1957. The building was not demolished until 1972, when the property became a parking lot.

Three large monuments in Old City Cemetery at 40th and Broadway mark the Reymershoffer families. A substantial rectangular monument remembers Gus's family while, across the walkway, John Jr. rests in peace beneath the prettiest memorial on Broadway: a gray granite stepped cenotaph topped with a kneeling woman.

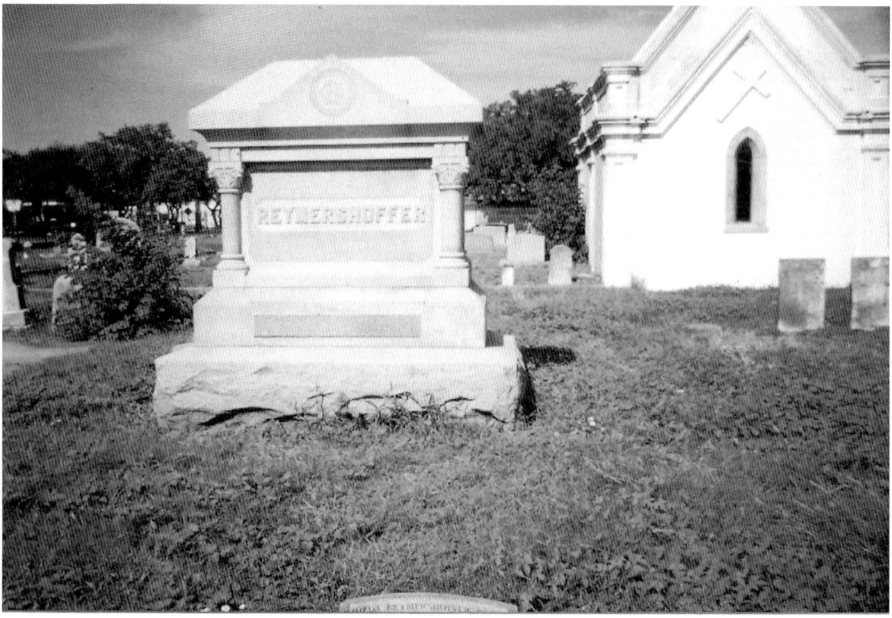

Headstone for the Reymershoffer family in Old City Cemetery, close to 40th and Broadway, within the Broadway Cemetery complex. *Author's collection.*

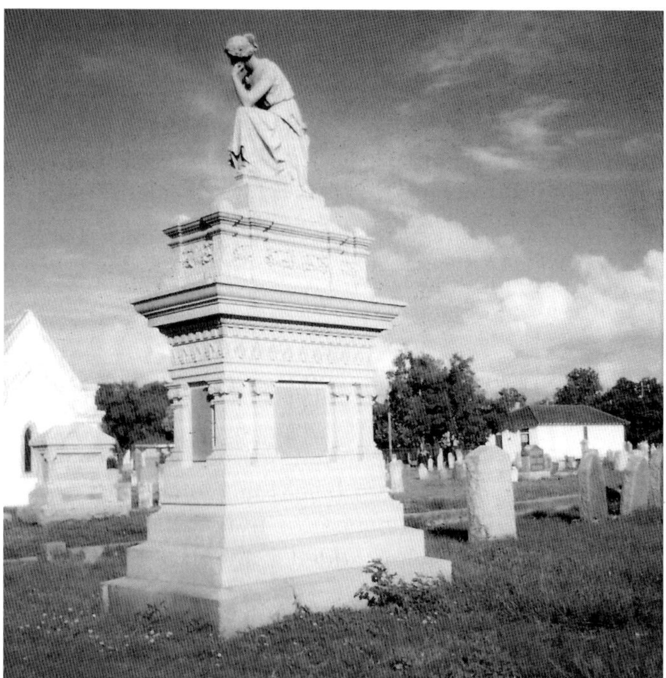

John Reymershoffer's monument is the most distinctive in the Broadway cemeteries' group of seven graveyards. *Author's collection.*

Galveston's "Music Men"

Among the Island city's long list of entrepreneurs were Islanders by Choice, Thomas, John and Mike Goggan (pronounced "gahgan"). They specialized in all things musical—from a wide variety of musical instruments to sheet music publication to piano assemblage.

Leading the way was Thomas Goggan. Born in Ireland in February 1843, he immigrated to the United States at age seventeen and first studied at St. Edwards University in Austin, Texas. After graduating from Springhill College in Mobile, Alabama, he moved to Galveston in 1866 with a complete stock of musical instruments to open the first music store in Texas: Thos. Goggan & Company, which was originally located in the old Tribune Building at 22nd and Postoffice.

Using the power of advertising, he placed his first ad in the *Dallas Herald* pronouncing himself a "Dealer in Sheet Music, Music Books, and all kinds of Musical Instruments." Two years later, his firm became the authorized agent for the *U.S. Musical Review*. He orchestrated a deal with the periodical that would spread his name—and reputation—statewide: he sent it the latest hits in sheet music, which the periodical published, acknowledging his company's contribution.

That same year, younger brother John joined the firm, and Thomas added the abbreviation "and Bro." to the firm's name. By 1868, the store had become the authorized dealer for Knabe pianos, as well as Steinway and Sons. Again Thomas turned to the power of advertising: beneath a banner broadcasting "Pianos! Pianos! Pianos!" he reminded clients that they could buy any one of them at 10 percent below factory prices.

His music store expanded its keyboard stock eight years later, requiring a larger store. Goggan chose a three-story brick building at 22nd Street and Market to house his growing inventory in 1877. Among the keyboard brands he sold were Peters, Webb and Company, Chickering and Sons, with pianos and organs by Mason and Hamlin, which sold for seventy-five dollars and ninety-five dollars, respectively. As for advertising, he changed his slogan to "Thos. Goggan and Bro.—Everything in Music."

When the market opened for musical instruments in other Texas cities circa 1880, the company added a shipping department, which brother John managed. The *Galveston Daily News* reported that Goggan "pianos were dragged across the plains of Texas in prairie schooners."

When their youngest brother, Mike, joined the firm as a clerk in 1880, Texas's first music man added an *s* to make Thos. Goggan and Bros. Three short years later, its first branch opened in San Antonio under Mike's management. Within five years, others had opened in Austin, Dallas, Waco, Houston, El Paso and Amarillo. The marching crescendo of their success spoke well for the power of advertising.

The Alamo City store, named the Goggan Palace of Music, became the firm's distribution center and hosted a "green room" for musical celebrities. By then, their inventory had grown to include accordions, violins, guitars and strings. Thomas Goggan announced his company as the largest piano and music house in Texas in all good conscience.

Despite its statewide presence, the company's headquarters remained at 22nd and Market on Galveston Island for forty-five years because that is where its founder lived. The 1880 census reported that Thomas lived with his wife, Annie, and five children—two daughters and three sons—at 1804 Church, built in 1886. Designed by Nicholas Clayton, it featured a double gallery crowned by a central gable with extensive gingerbread; it is still sitting behind its original cast-iron fence—all befitting Texas's first music man. After another girl was born, their family was complete at six.

Leaving the company in the capable hands of his brothers in 1880, Thomas was elected as county commissioner, choosing to perform his civic responsibilities. He composed frequent columns in local newspapers regarding various city political and social issues, such as repair and maintenance of the city's infrastructure, education and night schools. After Annie died on February 15, 1884, Thomas married Margarita the following year. Thirteen years later, he was elected police and fire commissioner.

Around the turn of the twentieth century, the music palace in San Antonio moved to Broadway and Travis. In addition to the sheet music and musical instruments, Mike's store added radios, phonographs and records along with all kinds of pianos—from uprights to grands, reproducing to player pianos.

An in-store brand of piano soon made its appearance: the "Goggan." In a common practice before World War I, music stores would merely stencil their names over a specially made named-brand instrument. Usually of poor quality, they were produced by companies such as Aeolian, Weber Piano and Pianola Company of New York. However, extant evidence—an inventory of made-to-order parts including cases, keys and actions—proved that Thos. Goggan and Bros. actually assembled its own pianos. Indeed, a piano of medium quality sporting the company's name cast (not merely stenciled) into its iron string-plate is still extant today, accompanied by a four-digit number.

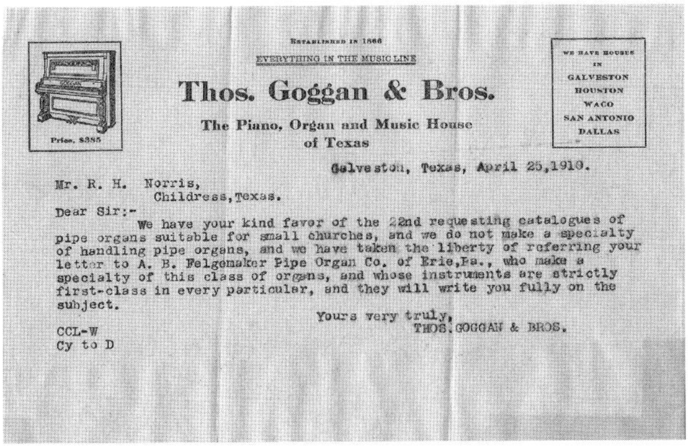
ESTABLISHED IN 1866

EVERYTHING IN THE MUSIC LINE

Thos. Goggan & Bros.

The Piano, Organ and Music House of Texas

Price, $385

WE HAVE HOUSES IN
GALVESTON
HOUSTON
WACO
SAN ANTONIO
DALLAS

Galveston, Texas, April 25,1910.

Mr. R. H. Norris,
Childress,Texas.

Dear Sir:-

We have your kind favor of the 22nd requesting catalogues of pipe organs suitable for small churches, and we do not make a specialty of handling pipe organs, and we have taken the liberty of referring your letter to A. B. Felgemaker Pipe Organ Co. of Erie,Pa., who make a specialty of this class of organs, and whose instruments are strictly first-class in every particular, and they will write you fully on the subject.

Yours very truly,
THOS.GOGGAN & BROS.

CCL-W
Cy to D

Carbon receipt of Thos. Goggan & Bros. referring Mr. R.H. Norris of Childress, Texas, to A.B. Felgemaker, Pipe Organ Company, Erie, Pennsylvania, postmarked April 25, 1910. *Author's collection.*

Thomas Goggan died on June 22, 1903, while visiting his Ireland home; however, six days later, the *Dallas Morning News* reassured clients that the music business continued to live on. Four years later, the company incorporated into two firms: Thomas's heirs would manage the Alamo City's Goggan Palace of Music, while John would oversee the Galveston store, as well as its Houston, Lufkin and Port Arthur branches.

Unfortunately, John died tragically during a Labor Day outing in 1908. A group of nineteen successful and respected Galveston businessmen planned a weekend campout on Redfish Reef. Perhaps in the midst of lively libation, several launched a small skiff for a late-night excursion on Saturday, September 5. An unexpected squall blew in, swamping the skiff near Camp Hughes and drowning both sixty-year-old Goggan and a retail grocer, John Moore.

The music man's obituary in the *Galveston Daily News* chronicled his life. Born in October 1847 in Tralee, County Kerry, Ireland, he immigrated to America in 1862. Moving from New York City to Cincinnati, Ohio, he worked for Peters Piano Company until he joined his older brother in Galveston six years later. The funeral for this "quiet, gentle music man" was held the following Tuesday at his residence, 1519 Avenue K, with his survivors listed as his widow, two daughters and two brothers—one living in Australia—with a sister back in Ireland.

Mike severed ties with Thos. Goggan and Bros. after his two brothers died to open his own music store in San Antonio. Goggan's Musical Goods, located at 225 East Houston, closed upon his death on November 26, 1914.

Both brothers' stores were still listed in 1914–15 *Texas State Gazetteer and Business Directory*. Mrs. John Goggan served as president of Thomas's firm, which was incorporated in 1907, while Thomas's son, Thomas S., was both vice-president and secretary.

One of Mrs. Goggan's daughters managed the Galveston store, which had moved across the street by 1929; a fire at its new location in July sent the company back to its previous address, 2124 Market. The company ceased to publish sheet music one year later, and Thos. Goggan and Bros.'s Galveston store closed in 1932, with all of its stock liquidated the following year. The Houston branch did remain open, but only until March 16, 1935, when the music died.

JUSTUS JULIUS SCHOTT: EXPERIMENTAL DRUGGIST

Under the threat of political punishment for supporting a united, democratic Germany, Justus and Louise Zeiss Schott left Kassel, Hesse. Together with their family of six, they arrived at Pier 20 in Galveston in 1851. At that time, half the city's population was German, so the wheelwright/carriagemaker settled in quickly, eagerly awaiting the beginning of their new lives in a new land.

At the time, middle son Justus was six years old. One day in secret, the young Schott walked to a slave block at 20th and Postoffice to watch the auction. Had his parents known, he certainly would have been in for a thrashing, as German immigrants opposed that "peculiar institution" of the American South.

Common on this Island paradise was the threat of yellow fever in the city, which rose up annually during the warm summer months. The disease began with cold-like symptoms and quickly progressed to jaundice, coma and internal bleeding. During the final state, a coffee-colored "black vomit" meant certain death. From 1839 through 1847, Galveston suffered three epidemics, which claimed the lives of more than 850 residents.

Momma and Papa Schott succumbed during a fourth breakout in 1853, leaving six orphans. Fortunately, neighbors Mr. and Mrs. J.H. Carstens adopted all of the children—Valentine, William, Henry, J.J., Catherine and Charles—expanding their already large family to eleven.

Justus attended elementary (or common) school in the home of a strict German schoolmaster for five years. As soon as he graduated at age thirteen, he went to work (in his brother's Henry's place) in a drugstore owned by George Behrman, Mrs. Carstens's brother. Over the years, young Schott learned the business from his druggist boss, who also taught him the mastery of thoroughness, sanitation and exactness in preparing the medications. Soon, Behrman grew to trust the boy to fill prescriptions correctly.

At the beginning of the Civil War, J.J. thought that he'd be required to attend military training for the Confederacy, but the captain took one look at his slight build and excused him based on health issues. Instead, the druggist-to-be returned to the store, watching the Battle of Galveston on January 1, 1863, from the docks as if it were a movie or TV show. When Behrman passed away later that year, Schott continued to manage the store for his heirs and, having served his apprenticeship, began earning a salary.

To help manage his money, he turned to Mrs. Carstens. After she deducted for his room and board, she doled out his weekly spending money of one or two dollars. What was left, she saved for him. By age nineteen, toward the end of the Civil War, Justus had hired his brother Charles to help him with the store.

The prevalence and frequent recurrence of yellow fever on Galveston Island persisted over the years, as both its cause and cure were unknown. With few trained doctors in the city and money scarce, druggists also assumed their responsibilities—compounding medicines from raw materials, dispensing it and offering advice on the various ills.

When J.J. turned twenty-one, Mrs. Carstens insisted that he move out on his own, so he took a room at the Old Washington Hotel. Around that same time, he bought the drugstore with the money she had saved for him, $1,000—just in time for another outbreak of yellow fever of 1867.

Despite J.J. Schott's best efforts, 1,150 Galvestonians succumbed to the disease that year, while more than 5,000, or one-third of the city's population, fled to Houston and the mainland. Two years later, while other doctors flocked to Galveston to study yellow fever, J.J. began experimenting with Mexican chicle for medicinal use.

A frequent drugstore customer, Captain Cook, ran the steamer *Annie Webber* between the Island and Tuxpam, Mexico. In 1869, he brought back a lump of chicle, which was used there for indigestion. Reasoning that what's good for the Mexicans would be good for Americans, he gave it to Justus to study.

Upon the public's initial rejection of the disagreeable stuff, the druggist began experimenting with methods to improve its flavor. He finally settled on a fixed process: first, he heated the chicle in hot water to remove its impurities, adding paraffin for consistency. To improve its taste, the druggist added sugar and flavorings, such as pineapple and wintergreen. Satisfied with his product, he gave away much more than he sold, selling the raw material wholesale to other druggists and the Wrigley gum manufacturer. By 1871, he had created a nationwide market and had also taken on two partners, Theodore Olmstead and a Mr. Thompson, into his new drugstore at 2011 Market.

In 1882, the Adams Chewing Gum Company sued Schott for $50,000 for patent infringement. In a New Orleans federal court, the Galveston druggist described the development of his process, which closely matched that of Adams but proved (with samples, pamphlets and notes) that his actually predated that of the company by five or six years. Although he could have pursued further litigation, he chose not to and eventually, sold his chewing gum process to Wrigley.

During this time, the druggist took a wife. In 1871, Justus Julius Schott married a farmer's daughter from San Antonio, Christine Rhode, on July 13. This began a marriage that would last fifty-seven years. They moved into a home at 1502 Postoffice, where both of their daughters were born.

By then, the couple could well afford to build a home on Broadway, which they did at no. 1809 in 1889. However, they did not build it for their family but rather as rental property. Although details are sketchy on its tenants, the house stayed occupied until fellow German Ferdinand H. Ohlendorf of Hanover bought it in 1920.

J.J. Schott died suddenly on May 6, 1928, at his home at 3619 Avenue R 1/2. The following day, the *Galveston Daily News* remembered him as "one of Texas' pioneer druggists," often ministering to "the afflicted." The paper cited that in its six decades of operation, his store had filled almost 1.5 million prescriptions. Following suit, the *Galveston Tribune* noted that "a long and useful life has ended," before it extended condolences "to the sorrowing survivors of this excellent man."

SAINTS AND SINNERS

Sainted Sanctuaries

Independence from Mexico in 1836 freed Texans to embrace Christian faith. Pioneer Galvestonians in particular sought spiritual strength to rise above the ever-present threat of death and destruction from the surrounding sea. Within two years of the city's founding in 1839, most of those denominations had established congregations or parishes on the Island. The oldest church on the Island is St. Mary's Cathedral, built in 1848; separate parishes soon followed.

Among the Protestants, Presbyterians led the way in January 1840, with the Lutherans following ten years later. Also during that time, both white Baptist and Methodist masters provided sanctuaries for their black slaves. After the Emancipation Proclamation took effect on June 19, 1865, in the Rebel states, these were deeded over to the new freedmen of color. The Jewish community established B'nai Israel in 1868, although Judaism was practiced in private homes as early as 1850.

With every faith of their city fathers working together, Galvestonians overcame many great calamities, especially the utter devastation of the 1900 Storm. Fifteen years later, they had built a seventeen-foot-tall seawall and literally raised the grade an average of eight feet in the East End for protection against future storms. As it grew, the city continued to make its mark on the state, the nation and the world through its visionary, humanitarian citizenry.

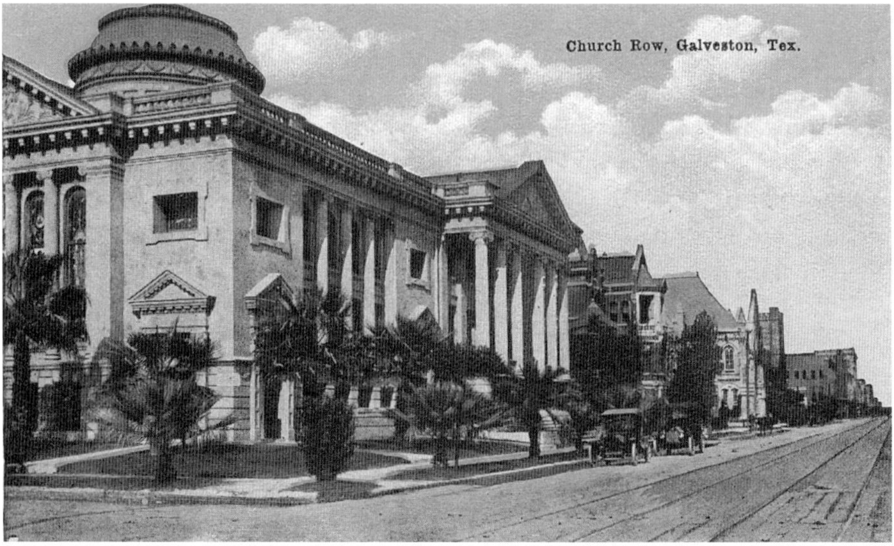

"Church Row," Twenty-Second Street north of Broadway. *Author's collection.*

You will find St. Mary's Cathedral (1847), Reedy Chapel (1886), Avenue L Baptist Church (1855), Sacred Heart (1884), the Ursuline Convent and St. Paul's United Methodist Church (1902) in *Walking Historic Galveston*. The driving guide includes First Presbyterian Church, the 1909 German Methodist Episcopal Church and the two cemeteries. Listed here are the seldom-seen sanctuaries, moving east to west.

TRINITY EPISCOPAL CHURCH, 701 22ND STREET

In January 1841, Reverend Benjamin Eaton came to Galveston to found the third Episcopal parish in Texas, expecting a tropical paradise. Instead, he was greeted by a chilling "blue norther." Undaunted by his initial disappointment, the Anglican priest held his first service on February 6, and Trinity Episcopal Church was born.

The present red brick Gothic Revival structure replaced a small wood-frame church that was heavily damaged during a storm in 1845, prompting plans for a new, larger church befitting the growing wealth and size of the city. Irish-born John de Young supervised the construction of John A. Fitzgerald's design at 22nd and Winnie, which was completed in 1857. Even though not structurally necessary, Reverend Eaton suggested the addition of large interior pillars to calm the fears of nervous worshipers and also conferred with the contractors to place a crypt beneath the altar for his final resting place.

On the morning of Palm Sunday, March 19, 1871, the reverend spoke with those who would take part in the pre-Easter pageant with an uncharacteristic frenzy, speaking to long-dead parishioners as if they were present. Gazing over his concerned congregation, he ascended his pulpit at the altar and began his sermon on the approach of Death, declaring that he saw the specter enter the front doors. Eaton reported its march up the broad aisle, passing over others, headed directly toward him. His voice trembling, he mumbled, "I am very sick but I must speak—to God the Father!" Then he collapsed into the arms of his friends, who bore him home. Reverend Benjamin Eaton died at 4:20 that afternoon, having served his congregation for thirty-three years. As he had requested, his body was entombed in concrete with a simple bronze plaque to mark his place. In 1926, when the church was raised four and a half feet, his tomb became a mausoleum in memory of all Trinity rectors.

Across the garth, Eaton Hall stands in tribute to Trinity's first rector, partially funded by Henry Rosenberg. The 1879 Victorian fellowship hall

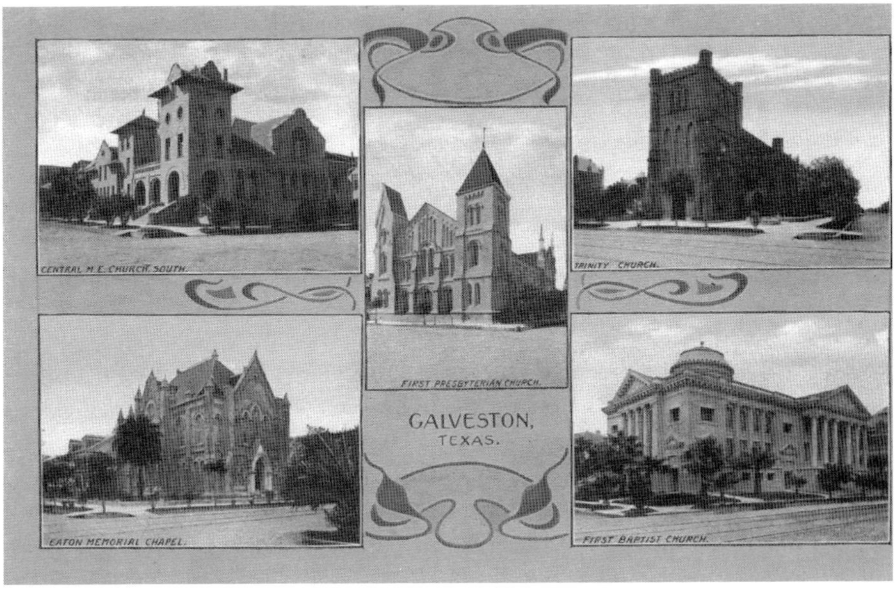

Galveston's five churches: Central ME South, First Presbyterian, Trinity, Eaton Memorial and First Baptist. *Author's collection.*

was designed by Nicholas Clayton, who was called on again to repair the 1900 Storm damage to the church's south wall. In 1904, he enlarged the west chancel above Trinity's altar to accommodate a large stained-glass window, "Christ and the Children," given in memory of George Sealy by his wife, Magnolia. Plans and funds to restore the window were already underway when Hurricane Ike struck on September 13, 2008. Unfortunately, all that was left of a middle panel were thousands of shards of glass. Craftsmen from the Willet Hauser Architectural Glass of Winona, Minnesota, carefully collected as many of them as they could salvage and painstakingly pieced the five-layer window back together, adding new glass as needed.

Congregation B'nai Israel, 816 22nd Street

Rosanna Dyer, the mother of the Texas Jewish community, was born in Galveston on February 26, 1809. She moved with her parents to Baltimore, where she met and married a merchant from Amsterdam, Joseph Ostermann, in 1825. Fourteen years later, they moved back to the fledgling Texas port city, where he sold his prosperous business to her brother, Isadore, and then retired. Judaism began as worship in his and other private homes on the Island. In 1852, Houston's Rabbi M.N. Nathan dedicated the Hebrew Benevolent Society located in the southwest corner of the Broadway cemetery.

After her husband died, Rosanna focused her attention on nursing victims of several yellow fever epidemics. Her home at 24th and Broadway served as a hospital during the Civil War, where she nursed both Rebels and Yanks. The city's first two-story residence, it became the YWCA in 1921.

On February 2, 1866, Mrs. Ostermann died quite unexpectedly during an explosion of the *W.R. Carter* on the Mississippi River. Among her many monetary gifts, she left $5,000 to build a synagogue on the Island and half that much to build one in Houston. Two years later, B'nai Israel had a rabbi of its own, with plans to build the new sanctuary.

As a charter was being secured from the Texas legislature, architect Fred S. Stewart laid the cornerstone for his Norman Gothic temple on June 9, 1870—the second temple in Texas. Seventeen years later, Nicholas Clayton designed a more ornate Victorian entrance. Included within its high-peaked gable surrounded by four slender turrets were the Tablets of Law, flanked by twin symmetrical wings; unfortunately, all the details have been stripped over the years. Adjoining the temple on its north side, a Community House, designed by Raymond Rapp in 1928, honored Rabbi Henry Cohen.

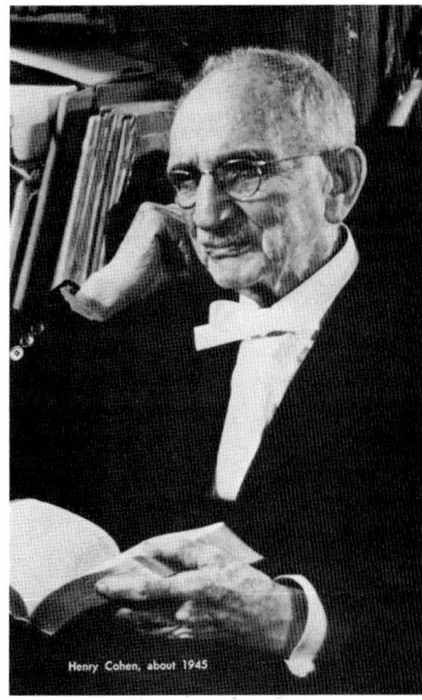

Rabbi Henry Cohen. *Courtesy of the Rosenberg Library, Galveston, Texas.*

Born in London, England, on April 7, 1868, Cohen came to Galveston in 1888 by way of Cape Town, South Africa; Kingston, Jamaica; and Woodville, Mississippi. Having been ordained four years earlier, Cohen was chosen to lead the 175 families of Congregation B'nai Israel, bringing Reform Judaism to the Island. One year later, he married Molly Levy, who raised two sons and daughter in the rabbinage at 1920 Broadway.

Hearing of the eastern European pogroms, Rabbi Cohen helped organize a worldwide syndicate, the Jewish Immigrants' Information Bureau, which relocated ten thousand Jews in America via the Port of Galveston. He served in the American Expeditionary Forces during World War I, during which time he persuaded Congress to provide Jewish naval chaplains. He was also one of the first to champion state prison reform.

In a comical *Mutt and Jeff*–style caricature, the mere five-foot-one Rabbi Cohen teamed with six-foot-three Monsignor James M. Kirwin to block the Causeway to stop the Ku Klux Klan from holding a cross burning on the Island, supported by hundreds of Galvestonians standing behind them. For fifty-seven years of his sixty-four years of service to the Jewish community, Rabbi Henry Cohen traveled the city streets on a bicycle, riding into Galveston folklore, coattails flying.

More opulent churches stood north of Broadway on 22nd Street, including both a Methodist and a Baptist house of God. Built in 1847 at 22nd and Sealy, a log cabin served as the First Baptist Church until a larger sanctuary complete with seven steeples was completed in 1883. Unfortunately, all were destroyed during the 1900 Storm. A domed Baptist church was dedicated in 1905 on the combined site and stood until 1962, when the present church, facing 23rd Street, replaced it.

St. Joseph's Church, 2202 Avenue K

Jean Marie Odin, born in Loire, was educated at the Sulpician seminary in Lyon, France. The last Vincentian in Texas, he came to Galveston in 1838 to manage the statewide diocese. Consecrated a bishop two years later, Bishop Odin oversaw the building of St. Mary's Cathedral and secured Catholicism in the state. Recognizing that German working-class immigrants represented half of Galveston's population, Bishop Odin ordained a parish for German-speaking Catholics in 1859, naming it after the patron saint of laborers, St. Joseph. Designed by architect Joseph Bleicke, this simple white wood-frame Gothic Revival church featured a square bell tower centered above the entry and was dedicated one year later. Inside you will find an ornate, hand-carved altar, crowned by a

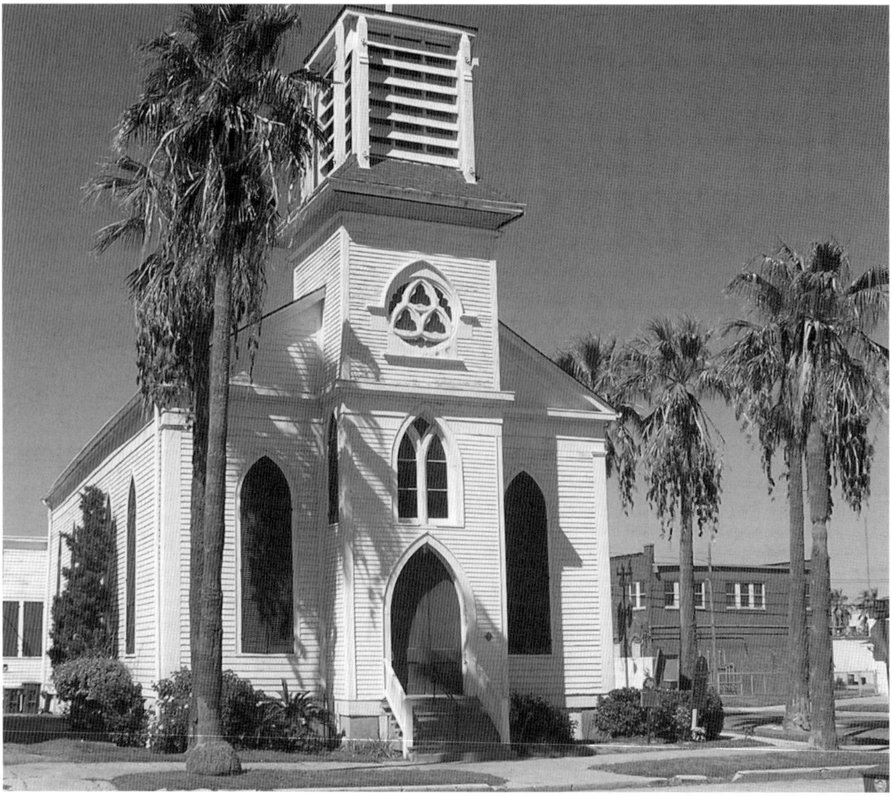

Erected in 1859 at 22nd and Avenue K, St. Joseph's served Galveston's German-speaking population of Catholics. *Author's collection.*

coffered ceiling painted in muted pastels with metallic gold five-pointed stars interspersed among Gothic symbols. As noted in the *Galveston Architecture Guidebook*, it "[g]alvestonize[d] the vernacular church type" in Texas, with its original cedar pews and plaster Stations of the Cross with German inscriptions. This church also operated the first parochial high school in Galveston from 1876 to 1926. After de-consecration in 1968, the Galveston Historical Foundation restored the sanctuary as a museum.

Galveston witnessed a succession of bishops who contributed to their faith and community. Recruited by seminary brother Odin, Louis Claude Marie Chambodut served as vicar general until ordained a bishop to supervise the building of St. Mary's hospital in the East End and orphanage on the beach in the West End, which was destroyed during the 1900 Storm (that dramatic story is in *Beyond the Beaten Paths*). Both were buried at the altar of St. Mary's Cathedral downtown, along with their successor. He served the diocese from 1882 to 1918, with his vicar general, James Martin Kirwin.

Born in Circleville, Ohio, Kirwin had come to Galveston four years before the 1900 Storm. He formed the Committee for Public Safety to provide oversight for relief efforts after the devastating hurricane. Almost blinded during a fire in 1901, the vicar general helped lay the cornerstone of Galveston's seawall the following year and then celebrated its completion to 23rd Street in 1904. Giving his permission to burn the victims' bodies, however, prevented him from ever becoming a bishop. Father Kirwin died on January 24, 1926, returning home for burial.

2127 Avenue K

Catty-corner from St. Joseph's stands a former corner store built in 1887. Across 22nd Street, note the two cottages, circa 1875.

2227 Avenue K

Early Galveston city father Lent Munson Hitchcock came to Galveston from Connecticut to join the Texas Navy in 1836. He married Emily Clifford three years later and bought a one-story Greek Revival house on the corner of 21st and Avenue K. A founding member of Trinity Episcopal Church, this harbormaster served eight terms as city alderman, four as treasurer and was a part owner of the Tremont Hotel. Attaining a net worth in 1860 of

$120,000, he invested in property throughout Galveston County. His widow moved to the mainland when he died in 1869. Six years later, she agreed to sell the Gulf, Colorado and Santa Fe Railroad a right-of-way only if it named a city after her late husband—Hitchcock, Texas, was born. Their Galveston home received a second story and porch circa 1880 and was then moved ten years later to 1111 22nd Street. Sold out of the family after the 1900 Storm, it was moved next door to its present location in 1964, finding its present address thirty-two years later.

2327 Avenue K

Waters Davis built this home for his daughter, Sarah, when she married Harry Hawley in 1907. Thirteen years later, they substantially remodeled it, lending it a timeless look.

Beth Jacob Synagogue, 2401 Avenue K

This temple was formed in 1930 when two Orthodox Jewish communities—one of Russian immigrants and the other Austro-Hungarian Jews—were united by one rabbi, Louis Feigon of Gastonia, North Carolina. The building, designed by Raymond Rapp, was dedicated on April 10, 1932, but was remodeled as an educational building when the present sanctuary was built in 1963. Ben J. Kotin and Tibor Beerman designed the project, which included the Bessie and Ben Clark Hall.

First Lutheran Church, 2415 Winnie

With the large number of Germans on the Island, a Lutheran place of worship soon became a necessity. In 1851, the Texas Synod was established in Galveston as the German Evangelical Lutheran Church. Six missionaries arrived from Basel, Switzerland, and one of them, Reverend Heinrich Wendt, became its new pastor. The congregation met at the small, red brick Lyceum Hall on the northeast corner of Winnie and Rosenberg; they bought it for $500 in 1855 and moved it across the street to the middle of the block.

Adjacent to the original Lyceum building, a white wood-frame meetinghouse was added thirteen years later at the corner of Winnie and 24th Street. Renamed the First Lutheran Church, this simple sanctuary sheltered many of the homeless after the 1900 Storm. In 1915, that sanctuary was raised and completely renovated, adding a Victorian corner tower, a bricked façade and stained-glass windows. Serving as the congregation's home until 1959, it has since been restored as a community center and, together with the adjacent building, renamed Lyceum Hall. Its current replacement, a most impressive Gothic limestone chapel, stands at the corner of 25th and Winnie.

Across Winnie on the corner, the Ladies Aid Society house was designed by Donald McKenzie in 1905, funded by a bequest from Henry Rosenberg's estate. Organized in 1882, its mission was to aid the poor, sick and unfortunate. This was extended to military personnel stationed in and around Galveston during World War I.

WESLEY TABERNACLE UNITED METHODIST CHURCH, 902 28TH STREET

Founded in 1869 by Reverend Peter Cavanaugh in a one-room house on Broadway, this African American congregation moved a former Presbyterian church from 14th Street, built in 1841, to this site in 1876. Norris Wright Cuney laid the cornerstone for the 1881 sanctuary that was destroyed during the 1900 Storm.

Black carpenter John Tankersley built a cottage-style sanctuary to replace it in 1901. Twenty-three years later, architects Stowe and Stowe raised that one-story church and constructed a new first floor, adding a corner tower, twin covered porches facing inward and a red brick façade. This combined the traditional roofline of the 1901 Gothic Revival cottage with the simpler Craftsman style of its newer first floor.

2901 Broadway

On the south side of Broadway stands the Van Alstyne House. Born in Houston in 1853, Albert Ashley Van Alstyne owned two steamboats berthed at Abraham Lufkin's Wharf at 25th Street. Six months after her father's death in 1877, Lufkins's daughter, Catherine, married Van Alstyne. In 1891, they built their impressive three-story Victorian home, featuring a towered catty-corner entrance near the city's western limits. Catherine continued to live here with her daughter, Mrs. Alverta V. Harvey, and grandchildren until her death in 1940. The house stayed in the family as rental property until new owners restored it in 1991.

Shiloh AME, 1310 29th Street

Originally the western outreach of Reedy Chapel at 20th and Broadway, trustees for the church bought this lot in 1870 for $500 but continued to worship in private homes until the loan was paid off. Named after the biblical city of Ephraim, which means "peaceable," they built two sanctuaries that were destroyed during two separate hurricanes. In 1923, the current building replaced the third, which proved to be poorly constructed, at a cost of $32,000. This figure included the pews and twenty-four stained-glass windows, designed and installed by the new Reverend L.M. Sanders.

Macedonia Baptist Church, 2920 Avenue M 1/2

As the city moved westward, Groesbeck's rural outlots were cut through east to west as needed, creating "1/2 avenues." However, the new streets' widths were not standardized. In this area, note that those avenues are more like one-car-wide alleys, giving the sanctuary a larger feel. Built in 1901, this Victorian church commands the area with its corner steeple. Note the 1927 Spiritual True Church across the street.

West Point Missionary Baptist Church, 3003 Avenue M

Crowned by an octagonal, golden cupola, this temple stands in stark contrast to the modest neighborhood around it. Although this black congregation dates to 1870 at 29th and Avenue R, the first official written records were dated 1882 and listed Reverend G.R. Cushenberry as pastor. After a move to

Broadway, West Point relocated to its present location in May 1900, housed in a small wood-frame structure. Work on the present two-story brick church began in 1916 under Reverend John C. Calhoun and was completed five years later by Fred Hadcock. Note its Greek Revival columns, repaired and renovated in 1970 to celebrate the congregation's centennial.

Malloy and Son Funeral Home, 3022 Broadway

British immigrant Frank P. Malloy established the company in 1902 in his livery stable at 24th and Postoffice, boasting the first horse-drawn ambulance. Within seven years, they had upgraded to a motorized ambulance and added the first automotive hearse in 1918. Architect Raymond Rapp studied funeral homes throughout the United States before designing its current facility. Note its many parlors that allow for multiple concurrent funerals. Taking four years to complete, the facility opened on August 16, 1930, as "the South's finest funeral establishment."

3112 Broadway

Two years earlier, in 1928, dry goods merchant Joe Eiband also hired Rapp to design his residence, which featured a circular driveway and wide front porch, giving a Mission-style appearance to the house.

CENTRAL METHODIST CHURCH, 3308 AVENUE O 1/2

This is the only historical church of this denomination left standing on the Island. The story of its presence, however, dates back to the beginnings of the state, as many Bible-carrying "circuit riders" called on early settlers.

Realizing the need for a Protestant house of worship, the Galveston City Company had given two lots on the northwest corner of 22nd and Avenue F (Church) in 1840. Reverend Thomas O. Summers traveled to Washington, D.C., to solicit a donation of $1,800 from Reverend William Ryland, the chaplain of the U.S. Senate. Named in honor of its chief financier, Ryland Chapel hosted its first service on June 24, 1843.

By 1869, the growth of the Methodist community had prompted the building of a larger and more beautiful brick sanctuary on the southwest corner of 25th and Broadway. St. John's Methodist Church featured a two-story, 110-foot Gothic bell tower east of its entry, with an alcove for the pulpit inside at the rear of the building.

Three years later, demand for a church farther east prompted dry goods businessman David Ayres, a former circuit rider, to endow St. James Methodist; his wife donated land at 14th and Avenue E (or Postoffice). Another large gift completed the edifice in 1883. The first Texan elected Methodist bishop, Seth Ward, served as pastor from 1887 to 1889. Unfortunately, both of these sainted sanctuaries were destroyed during the 1900 Storm.

Again, Dr. Ward was called to supervise the consolidation of the two congregations this time. A small wooden structure held services until a grander, Mission-style church was completed on the corner of 19th and Sealy in 1901. Designed by George B. Stowe, it featured a somewhat awkward Spanish architecture with small towers and low oval windows. The transom over its southwest corner entrance proclaimed it the "Central Methodist

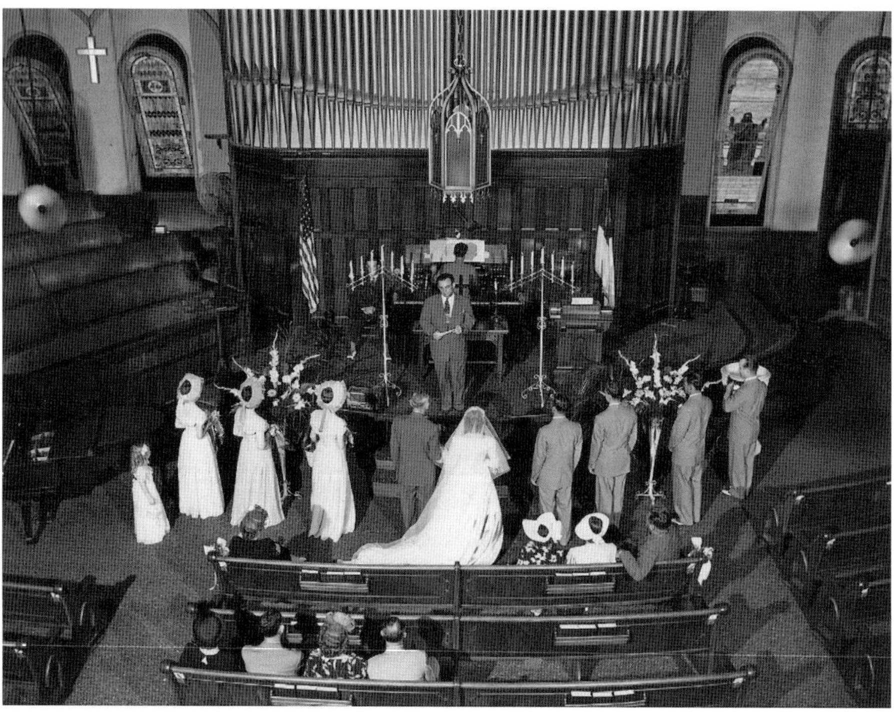

Interior, Central ME South. *Author's collection.*

Episcopal Church, South, of Galveston," as did its cornerstone. As a symbol of unification, the cornerstones of both St. John's and St. James were also installed in its foundation. In 1906, its name was changed to the First Methodist Church, making this sanctuary one of a kind—having three cornerstones, none of which sported its actual name. The building was torn down during the 1950s.

West of the city proper, Sunday school Methodist missions met in various homes and buildings beginning in 1885. After it secured a building at 39th and Sealy, the West End Methodist Church was officially organized three years later. Its present location at 33rd and Avenue O 1/2 was decided on in 1915 and a temporary tabernacle was built. It was renamed Central Methodist Church on December 22, 1927, and several more buildings completed the complex from the 1930s to the 1950s.

In her will, Libby Shearn Moody endowed a new Methodist church to be built at 53rd and Avenue U. Designed by Mark Lemmon of Dallas, the cathedral-like Moody Memorial First Methodist Church held its first service on February 16, 1964. It is well worth a short drive to see this complex, which includes a large, modern community building and a senior citizens care facility called Libby's Place.

1013–27 34th Street

Note the tall tower of St. Patrick's Catholic Church as you drive west on Broadway. As the city moved west, Bishop Claude Dubuis established a parish at this location in 1870, naming it after the patron saint of Ireland. Founding member and Irishman Nicholas J. Clayton built a two-story frame church that was unfortunately destroyed in a storm the night before the new pastor arrived from Indianola. Picking up the pieces, Father Lawrence Glynn laid the cornerstone on March 14, 1872, for a massive thirteenth-century ornate Gothic Revival structure that he would not live see to completion twenty-six years later. Completed in 1895, its final phase was a 205-foot spire, topped by a Celtic cross and dedicated to the city's founder, Michel Menard. During the 1900 Storm, that tower fell down backward and destroyed the roof and interior of the sanctuary—talk about the "luck of the Irish." For a third time, Clayton was chosen to rebuild the present sanctuary, which was completed in 1905. The current tower, standing only 120 feet high, was not completed until 1922.

BROADWAY BAPTIST CHURCH, 3501 BROADWAY

Reverend Robert D. Wilson organized this African American church in 1910. C.W. Bulger and Son designed and built the church four years later, but it was partially destroyed during the 1915 hurricane. Czech Rudolf Mudrak, who came to Galveston as an administrative employee of the St. Louis architectural firm of Mauran and Russell—builders of the Hotel Galvez—constructed a modification of Bulger's design that was razed by fire one year later. Mudrak continued the project until the present building was completed 1917, which included fifty-five green "glass art windows."

1015 35th Street

Directly behind the church stands a cottage built in 1873 by Sydney Martin, who worked for the commission firm of P.J. Willis. Martin sold this part of his homestead to W.G. Belding in 1876. By 1910, it was serving as the parsonage for the church on Broadway, now called Sunlight Baptist.

1019–21 35th Street

Also built by Martin in 1873, this once simple Greek Revival home was substantially remodeled in 1876 by its next owners, Ella and Joseph G. Goldthwaite. She was the daughter of P.J. Willis.

1115 35th Street

A salesman for P.J. Willis, Joseph J. Hunter hired Robert B. Garnet to build this house in 1877. Note the mansard roof of this raised cottage.

1205 35th Street

On this site, General Thomas N. Waul built a southern townhouse in the 1860s. When architect and master builder Nicholas J. Clayton brought his mother from Cincinnati circa 1874, he bought the small raised cottage on the southeast corner at 3527 Avenue L. He lived here with her until he married the younger Lorena Ducie in 1892, at which time he also bought the Waul home. Since the architect was facing bankruptcy, lawyer Joseph Franklin advised him to tear down the fence between the two so that he could claim the full half block as his homestead—something the stubborn Clayton refused to do. After he passed in 1916, his widow continued to raise their five children here until her death in 1944; the house was torn down two years later. Some of Clayton's descendants had already moved to La Marque in 1938 while daughter Mary moved her photography studio to 1516 Market, leaving the little cottage catty-corner from the Grace Episcopal Church for others to live in.

GRACE EPISCOPAL CHURCH, 1115 36TH STREET

The parish was originally founded by Trinity Episcopal Church as a Sunday school outreach in 1874 for Galveston's growing west-side community. Two years later, the self-supporting congregation established a church of its own with a gift from Henry Rosenberg's estate. A small original wood-frame chapel was moved from the corner circa 1894 to make way for that new stone sanctuary. Built in 1895, this simple, Leon limestone sanctuary was designed by Nicholas Clayton.

Until 1884, the Rosenberg household had been very active in Trinity, with Henry serving as vestryman for twenty years. A disagreement in policy—to robe the choir—precipitated the departure of the wealthiest family in the city to its western outreach, even though it meant traveling farther from their home at 13th and Market. That household included Henry, wife Letitia and her younger childhood friend Mollie Ragan MacGill. At Letitia's invitation, Mollie visited Galveston in 1856 from Hagerstown, Maryland; however, her family moved to Richmond, Virginia, during the Civil War, during which time she nursed Rebel soldiers to honor their Confederate sympathies.

As soon as the war ended, Mollie again moved in with the Rosenbergs to nurse her ailing friend, Letitia. The two women's strong bond grew to include the man over twenty-two years. When Letitia passed in June 1888, the couple waited the proper year and a half of Victorian mourning before they married. The couple visited his original Switzerland home before Henry passed away in 1893. Without an heir, his estate, which was valued at more than $1 million, was parceled out for very specific projects around the Island. One of them was Grace Episcopal; its ornate interior, however,

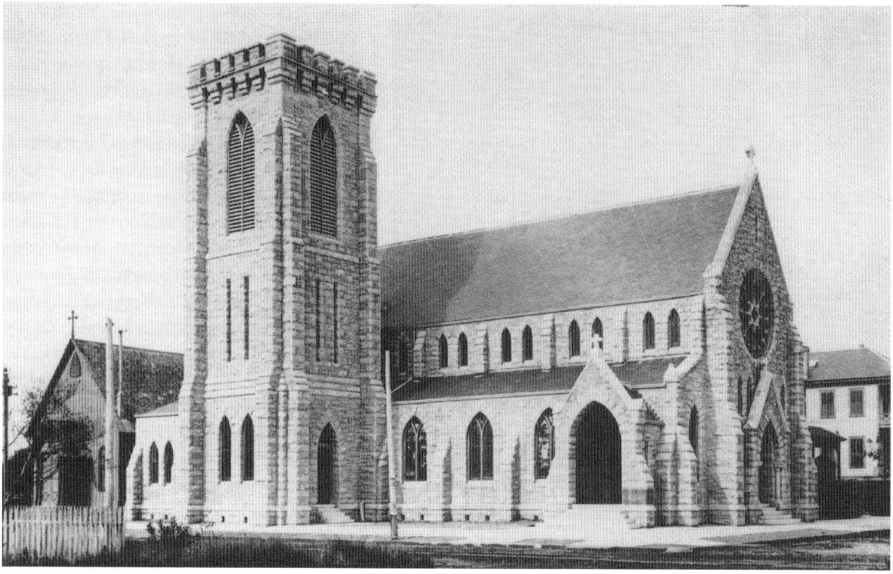

Grace Episcopal, 36th and Avenue L. *Courtesy of James Anderson.*

was a gift from the second Mrs. Rosenberg. In addition, "Aunt Mollie," as she became known, provided deep pockets to take care of the church that her Henry had built until she died in 1917.

With Henry in mind, she chose a simple, pointed, Gothic design for its exterior that incorporated elements of High Victorian style. Constructed completely of Texas white Leon limestone, it included a carriage entrance and square bell tower on its south side. When it was consecrated on November 17, 1895, the *Galveston Daily News* reported, "It was the custom in olden times to give the finest and most magnificent to God, to dedicate the richest personal gifts to his service that men might be better. True to this ideal, Grace Church has been raised from the earth that God has created to mount toward the heavens as far as human hands, in their weaknesses, can go."

Opening the double entry doors, painted red to symbolize the blood of Christ, one can view Grace's richly appointed interior, designed by Silas McBee. Crowned by a dark wood open-truss ceiling resembling the hull of a ship, the hand-carved altar and canopied partition behind the altar (or reredos) were oak, believed from Switzerland. A prevailing custom for craftsmen at the time, a planned imperfection on the reredos (the misspelling of the word *sacrifice*), signified that only God is capable of perfection. On either side of the chancel railing, a brass pulpit and bronze statue of Gabriel (a gift from Mollie "in loving memory of my dear friend Letitia") came from New York. The dark wood sharply contrasted with the original multicolored, multi-shaped stained-glass windows, all reflecting the role of women in Christianity. The wheel window above the entry depicted the sacred musical images from Psalm 150, as the late afternoon sun cast its colors across the altar every day.

Outside the sanctuary in the cloister garth stands a giant Japanese yew tree. In 1983, the winds of Hurricane Alicia blew down the immature tree, completely uprooting it. Using a winch truck, determined parishioners painstakingly set it up right to its full height and secured it so it could root again. Growing even stronger, fuller and taller, Grace's sheltering yew, proclaimed the largest of its kind in the state by the Texas Forest Service, serves as a parable for the quaint limestone church that survived and thrived despite the odds.

During Hurricane Ike in September 2008, the church flooded two to three inches—just enough to restore the floor and original pews. The congregation first removed the latter, sending them away for restoration. It then removed the old, red, nasty indoor/outdoor carpet, threadbare in places, to find a layer of linoleum glued to the original floor. After scraping that up, parishioners revealed the dark hardwood floor matching the ceiling, which was refinished to its original glory.

1124 37th Street

At the corner of 37th Street behind the church is an 1867 southern townhouse. Dating to the beginning development of the city's West End, the home was constructed for Dr. and Mrs. Lafayette Garrett. Note its Greek Revival–like columns and flat roof. Now called the Silk Purse, it is a resale shop owned by Grace Episcopal. The wooden sculpture of the angel and lambs, carved by Earl Jones, also belongs to the church. The site of several large plantations, many of the homes in this Old Central area along Avenue M also date from the early settlement of the West End.

The next residence is located at 39th and Avenue P, aka Count Bernardo de Galvez Avenue, named for the Spanish viceroy who commissioned a survey of the Island and the bay in 1784. Although both bear his name, De Galvez never visited the area, as two years before the survey was completed, he died at age forty of yellow fever in New Orleans.

3827 Avenue P

Born in Norwich, New York, on January 28, 1804, Thomas Henry Borden joined Stephen F. Austin's "Old Three Hundred" in 1824. His older brother, Gail, followed him to Texas five years later and succeeded him as Austin's official surveyor. Both had moved to Galveston before the state's War for Independence. Thomas helped lay out the city of Houston in 1836, while his brother sold 2,500 lots for the Galveston City Company. On January 30, 1840, Reverend James Huckins met with nine charter members in this house to establish the First Baptist Church.

Gail and his wife, Penelope, were the first to be baptized in the Gulf of Mexico five days later. The church itself was subsequently built in the city's downtown. Finding his calling as an inventor while on the Island, he moved to New York to patent his process for condensed milk in 1856.

Thomas chose to stay in Galveston to farm and invent, even though he owned much land in Fort Bend and Brazoria Counties. He built the first windmill and invented a gauge for steamboats. Some even think that he also built the terraqueous machine that traveled on both land and sea that was often attributed to his older brother. Not believing in the power of patents, however, Borden died rather destitute on March 16, 1877. A 1936 monument from the Texas Historical Commission in his honor faces 39th Street.

3815 Avenue P

Next door, almost hidden behind an iron fence and trees, stands a 1928 design by Houston architect John Staub. Built for cotton exporter William C. Helmbrecht, the rather austere orange, black and yellow brick house features two small oval windows on either side of the front door, with louvered blinds surrounding both door and windows.

SIN CITY OF THE SOUTHWEST

What manner of man molded the character of Galveston before the city's official founding in 1839? Unfortunately, it seems that this barrier island in the Gulf of Mexico attracted the dregs of humanity to its shores: heathens, harlots, reprobates, cutthroats, libertines, criminals and rogues—all bringing the seven deadly sins with them.

Its first inhabitants were the Karankawas, a band of primitive, nomadic Indians that originated from the Carib tribe. Making their way to Galveston during the 1400s, they lived on the mainland during the cold winter months and vacationed on the Island in summer, where they would hunt and fish. Even though they had strong familial traditions, they defended their territory according to the paternalistic "Cult of the Warrior." In ritualistic ceremonies, they would roast those they vanquished on a blazing bonfire and consume them piece by piece to suck up the strength of their enemies.

In 1528, ninety survivors of Pánfilo de Nárvaez's expedition washed ashore on the Island, emaciated and near death. Thanks to the compassion of the pagan Indians, most of the Spanish survived the shipwreck; however, that first harsh winter decreased their number to four. Their leader, Cabeza de Vaca, named the inhospitable harbor "La Isla de Malhado" (translated "Island of Misfortune") before escaping on foot. The Karankawas were left with two hundred years of privacy—until pirates moved in.

Exiled from Louisiana in 1816, corsair Jean Lafitte sailed his freebooters west along the Gulf Coast to discover a natural port on a bay—the perfect homeport for his new slave trade. He promptly set up shop in his second pirate colony on the Island's East End, between 14th and 15th Streets on what is now called Harborside Drive. Then it was back to business as usual.

At its height, his settlement boasted 120 buildings (including obligatory saloons and whorehouses with gaming pursuits), with a pirate population of two thousand, all lead by Lafitte as judge, jury and executioner. By 1820, however, his men's eyes had turned westward toward the comely Indian maidens, and a small bank of buccaneers kidnapped and raped one of the Karankawa women. As revenge, the warriors killed four of the freebooters in the first battle ever fought on Galveston Island. For three days, the Indians fought the pirates, but bows and arrows were no match for muskets and cannons.

During the next twenty years of colonization, cannibals and pirates gave way to land speculators and entrepreneurs, many on the run from their previous lives, who carved out a new republic along with its commerce capital. With conflicting governance, they made up the rules as they went along, living on their word and reputations. Fortunately, it turned out well for all.

After the Civil War, Galveston's natural harbor grew quickly into the world's third-largest seaport for cotton exports. Its waterfront "sawdust" saloons on the Strand became known worldwide as wild drinking and gambling establishments where they swept out various body parts the mornings after, no questions asked.

Equally infamous were the *nymphs de pave* of the brothels that lined Postoffice Street west of 25th Street, a segregated red-light district that operated openly since the beginnings of the city in the 1830s and continued until the mid-twentieth century. During 1929 alone, it was estimated that eight to nine hundred ladies of the evening worked the Island's houses, making much better money than any legitimate working girl.

Recognized as a commodities market destination, the Island city attracted the likes of transient workers such as cotton wagoners, draymen, drovers, merchant seamen and stevedores. This all-male population was usually paid in lump sums for their weeks or months of hard work; sharp businessmen (and women) merely gave them the opportunities to appease their appetites in the form of sex, liquor and risk. By applying a basic law of business—supply and demand—everyone was satisfied: working men spent their days and cash as they wanted, while bar owners, bookies, madams and their girls collected it.

Writer-historians coined the name "Free State of Galveston" to describe the era from Prohibition to the mid-'50s, when all manner of sin drove the city's economy. Local civic leaders and law enforcement of this insular community adopted a "live and let live" attitude toward the flourishing vice industry because it was prosperous, exciting and slightly risqué—all of the activities that were illegal everywhere else.

Not really being *in* Texas but merely located *near* it (situated 2.5 miles off its coast) provided just enough distance from reality, necessary for prostitution, drinking and gambling to be acceptable, even out in the open. "The general attitude of the island was one of independence," wrote David McComb in his book *Galveston: A History*. "[T]he people who lived there…had been through hell and high water, and survived.…They broke the laws, natural and human, and got away with it."

BARBERS TO BOOTLEGGERS TO BOOKIES

On September 8, 1900, the worst natural disaster swept clean the most populous parts of Galveston, forever altering the destiny of this port city. During its recovery, the Lucas gusher blew in one year later at Spindletop (about one hundred miles northeast of the Island), and the Houston oil industry was born. To transport the "black gold," the Bayou City dug its ship channel (aka the "Big Ditch," as Galvestonians called it), which opened in 1914, taking business and industry away from the Island. A return to its economic roots was necessary—only much grander, and with the right men to make it happen.

The same year as Spindletop, the Maceo family immigrated to Louisiana from Palermo, Sicily. By the time the Houston Ship Channel had opened, brothers Salvatore ("Sam") and Rosario ("Rose") were living on Galveston Island. Barbers by trade, Sam, the charmingly handsome younger brother, cut hair at the new, fashionable Hotel Galvez on the Seawall, while his rougher-spoken brother set up shop downtown at the Turf Athletic Club. At a quarter per head, success came slowly, until a law offered opportunity.

Prohibition came to Texas in 1918 when the state legislature ratified an amendment declaring all alcohol illegal. Two years later, the Volstead Act ensured that the nation would follow suit. In defiance, some folks started making homebrew and bathtub gin. Most, however, resorted to widespread bootlegging—the illicit manufacture or distribution of liquor, originating from the American frontier practice of smuggling concealed flasks of whiskey in boot tops when trading with the Indians.

The irony of this "Noble Experiment" was that *more* liquor was consumed as a new crime emerged: nationwide, illegal syndicates formed to supply the demand for illegal booze. Sam and Rose's illegal empire was just one of them.

Galveston Island was ideally suited, with its twenty miles of undeveloped beach on the Gulf Coast in the West End—truly a rumrunner's dream. "Dutch" Voight and his Beach gang hired the barber brothers to bring in, hide and distribute contraband liquor from Havana, Bermuda, Europe or South America to Ollie Quinn's downtown speakeasies.

Once identified through the sliding Judas-hole of a locked door to the speakeasies and admitted, most people were up for a little illegal gambling; as the "smart" thing to do, it didn't really hurt anyone. In the flapper era, forbidden was fun. Occasionally, raids took place, but they were more for show for the newspapers than serious cleanup efforts. Gaming downtown grew to include slot machines, keno, tip books, monte, bingo and lotteries. Big-league gambling was there too: roulette, poker and betting on sporting events at the Turf Athletic Club on Market between 22nd and 23rd Streets.

With the money they made from bootlegging, the Maceos expanded into the nightclub business, partnering in 1926 with the gang and gambler Jackie

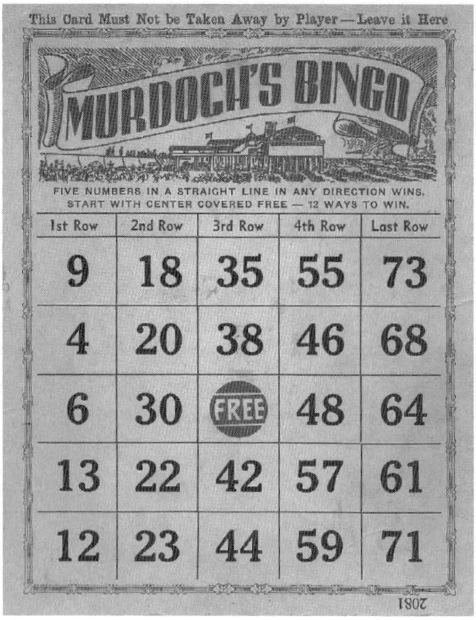

Left: Murdoch's Bingo card. *Author's collection.*

Below: The sign on top of the Balinese Room pointed toward the Turf Athletic Club, which was downtown just west of 21st Street between 22nd and 23rd Streets on Market (Avenue D). Both were the Maceos' gaming establishments.

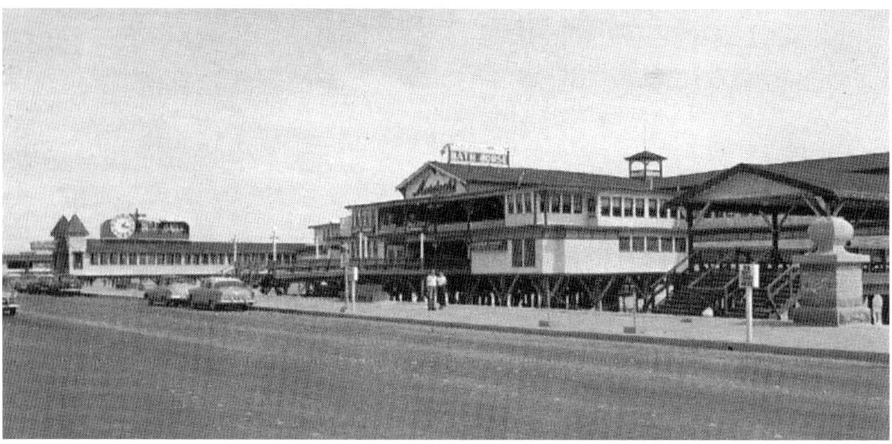

Friedman to open an exclusive "speak": the Hollywood Dinner Club. Located on the western outskirts of the city at 61st Street and Stewart Road, the HDC quickly became nationally recognized as the first of its kind, offering gourmet dining, drinking, dancing to top-name Hollywood entertainment and, if you knew whom to ask, a little illegal gambling in its ultra-private back room. In another first, it was air-conditioned. Manager Sam insisted that it be kept cool enough so that "the clientele don't 'feel' the booze." (Friedman soon sold out to the Maceos to open the Sands in Las Vegas, bringing the Galveston ambiance to the up-and-coming desert resort.)

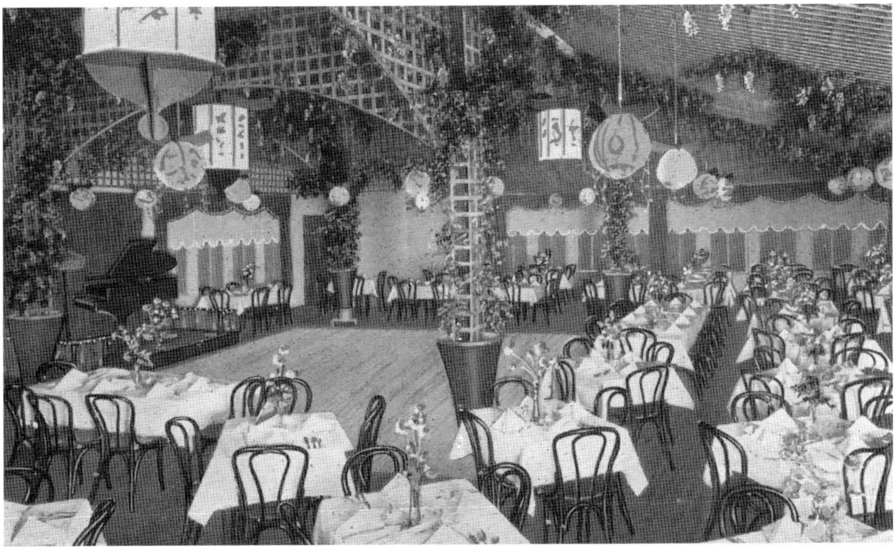

Chop Suey Café (renamed Balinese Room in 1942). *Author's collection.*

On the seawall at 21st Street, the Maceos bought a restaurant on a fishing pier just over the Gulf of Mexico and across the street from the Galvez Hotel. Originally called the Grotto, they converted it into a second speakeasy/supper club in 1925, renaming it the Chop Suey.

A storm heavily damaged it in 1932, and while repairs were underway, Sam just happened upon General John J. Pershing's personal Chinese chef, Go-Bo. Maceo then imported him to the Island to cook his favorite cuisine, naming his new restaurant Sui Jen (pronounced "swee-wren"), which means "Dine and Dance" in Chinese. Its Asian décor included "the South's loveliest dance pavilion," which featured a pagoda bandstand, which soon grew famous for its Tokio Ballroom, dining, dancing and high-stakes gaming.

THE THIRD COAST

By 1932, the Maceos had cornered the market on vice in Galveston County. Their Gulf Vending Company ensured that their 50/50 take slot machines sat in businesses, while their clubs consolidated under the Turf Athletic Club Syndicate, located downtown at 2214 Market. With a public bookmaking parlor on the ground floor, the second floor was reserved for two private clubs: the cowboy-inspired Western Room and Art Deco Studio Lounge. The actual athletic club, storage and the syndicate's office filled the top floor. In some circles, it became known as the unofficial "Weekend Bank of Galveston."

Prohibition officially ended on December 6, 1933, and beer, whiskey and hard liquor could be bought by the bottle at stores. However, liquor sold by the drink remained illegal in Texas for another forty years. "Games of chance" were still illegal, too, but by then Maceo and Company had become an established Galveston institution, mixing glamour with gambling to accommodate those in search of a little action.

The ten years from 1932 to the end of 1941 were hard years for the U.S. economy. The Great Depression stretched from the Atlantic coast to the Pacific coast; between 13 and 15 million people were unemployed. Franklin Delano Roosevelt, then governor of New York, pledged a New Deal for the American people who elected him president of the United States.

On America's third coast, the Gulf of Mexico, the economy was going strong—a "new deal" took place every few minutes when the blackjack tables were open. Few people were out of work, as the Maceos' holding company, Gulf Properties, employed more than 2,500 people—about 10 percent of Galveston's population, according to author Gary Cartwright. This didn't include those police, judges and politicians who were "off the payroll," so to speak.

While banks closed in thirty-eight states, Sam could walk into any bank on the Island, borrow $100,000 on his signature alone and pay it back in two weeks at 25 percent interest. In 1934, Sam "Books" Serio became the accountant and financial advisor for Maceo and Company. When questioned about the Depression years, he replied, "You couldn't tell it down here. Money was flying all over the place!"

Papa Rose ran the Island with a no-nonsense business attitude. While Mr. Roosevelt insisted that "the only thing we have to fear is fear itself," fear was kept off the streets by the Maceos' private police force. "Rose's Night Riders" patrolled Galveston's downtown club areas, offering big winners safe rides back to their hotel. Cheating and stealing were rare at the casinos, and the clubs were never robbed. Rose also saw to it that all games were kept "on the square." Long before Las Vegas, they learned that the percentage is always with the house. Any rumor of a crooked game might keep Texas oil and stockmen millionaires away and must be dispelled immediately. When the nationwide mafia threatened to invade their turf, he told their representatives, "Get on the Causeway…and don't come back." And they didn't.

Raids became routine and polite with local city and county police. The cops would call the TAC offices, usually around holidays, and say, "We caught you. Come on down to the station and pay your fine." The accountant "Books" Serio would oblige, wishing the cops a "Merry Christmas" or "Happy Fourth of July" with a few cases of top-shelf whiskey. Other raids were conducted so local politicians could get their names and pictures in the newspapers at election time.

To put these numbers in perspective: for $0.05 in 1933, grandpa could buy a pack of cigarettes or a bottle of beer, fill up his coupe with gas or take two pulls on a bell-fruit-gum slot machine. Based on the Consumer Price Index (CPI), $1.00 spent then had the same buying power as $10.89 in 1995—that's a lot of cigarettes, beer and gasoline for $0.30.

THE INFAMOUS BALINESE ROOM

The Texas Rangers, made part of the Department of Public Safety in 1936, did not cooperate well with local law officials. Wearing their customary ten-gallon white cowboy hats, they proved inhospitable to the Maceos when they raided and closed down the Hollywood Dinner Club three years later. Rumors were that the rangers planted narcotics on the premises because they couldn't make a bona fide gambling bust.

Moving the HDC operation to the seawall, Sam spent a year painstakingly remodeling both the Turf building downtown and the Sui Jen, the latter by adding a three-hundred- to four-hundred-foot walkway over the Gulf with a T-head on the back. Pearl Harbor in early December 1941, however, forced a change in his planned Asian décor to an exotic Polynesian style. Renaming it the Balinese Room, the dining room featured hand-painted wall murals of Island girls dressed in pink against bright-green topical beaches. No "grind joint," everything here was first class.

The long promenade (soon to be known as "Ranger's Run") was decorated with glass ball floats, fishing nets, palm trees, aquariums and plush carpet. It served as a buffer zone between the seawall and its private casino. To get there, "members" and their guests would be cleared at the front door and then walk down the angled pier to the main dining room and then through

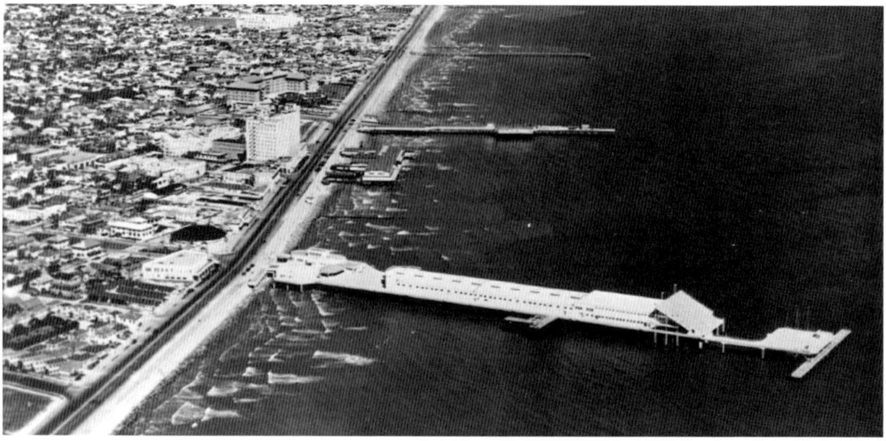

Seagull's-eye view of the Pleasure Pier, at 25th Street, and a beachfront view also showing Murdoch's and the Balinese Room, the Buccaneer and Hotel Galvez. *Author's collection.*

the restaurant and across the ballroom floor to the bar, with a final clearance to gain entrance into the casino.

Catering to the rich high rollers and well-heeled patrons of the medical and oil industries in Houston and Dallas, the Balinese opened on January 17, 1942, as Sam Maceo invited all to "Come Down and Play" on Galveston Island. Legendary entertainers there included Phil Harris, Jack Benny, Gene Autry, Frank Sinatra, Tony Bennett, Joe E. Lewis, Frankie Lane, the Ritz brothers, Bob Hope, George Burns and Gracie Allen, Sophie Tucker and Victor Borge. Several stars would even stage free outdoor shows on the seawall on Sunday afternoons, attracting an audience of up to twenty thousand. When the newly air-conditioned Pleasure Pier reopened in 1949, knot-headed Charlie McCarthy with his voice, Edgar Bergen, served as Mardi Gras King.

Even though the entertainment cost upward of $18,000 to $20,000 per week for name bands and acts, that investment was more than made up at the gaming tables, which numbered two roulette wheels, two blackjack tables and three dice tables (one for $1 to $25 bets, a second for $5 to $200 bets and a table that ran $500 to $2,500 bets).

The dollar figures after the B'room opened were even more impressive. One of its $500 gaming chips in 1942 would equal $5,045 in the 1995 market. At the same time, whenever a high-rolling craps player bet $100,000 on one toss of the dice, the 1995 CPI equivalent was $760,680. Although individuals were on the syndicate's payroll, very little of this cash went into the city's coffers.

Despite this, the Maceos shared their wealth through their generous donations to many and various causes on Galveston Island. Miraculously, whenever priests played at their tables, they won. When churches and other charities fell short on their fundraisers, a single donation from the Turf Athletic Club suddenly surpassed all goals. Many young men of modest means graduated college on the brothers' dime. In 1947, when the Texas City dock blew up twice within twenty-four hours, Sam reached out to his Hollywood entertainment friends to perform pro bono in several benefits for the victims. General admission tickets cost ten dollars per person as headliners like Jack Benny and Rochester, George Burns and Gracie Allen and a rather drunk Frank Sinatra took the stage, filling the City Auditorium to the rafters.

In short, Sam and Rose Maceo "adroitly achieved an aura of legitimacy and respectability while conducting an illegitimate and illegal business," according to *Houston Post* reporter Harold Scarlett. Even though everyone knew that illegal gambling was wide open on the Island, no authority would do anything about it.

THE BEGINNING OF THE END

In 1956, however, Will Wilson was elected attorney general on a pledge to "close down Galveston" using the Texas Rangers. By the time the Rangers had entered from the seawall and run the length of that long promenade, through the supper club, dance floor and bar, all guests were merely dining, dancing and drinking, with no evidence of gambling in sight.

According to retired B-Room croupier Al Parsuitt, the pit bosses knew that the "trip took at least 2 minutes for the fastest Ranger, but we could shut down in 1 minute, 15 seconds" in a well-choreographed routine. During a raid, everyone had a job to perform, according to a highly choreographed strategy. At the craps table alone, the box man would push the check rack to the center of the layout, while the dealer took off the table side racks and put them on top of the rack, with the stick on top of that. Each guy would fold a corner of the layout into the middle. The whole bundle would be picked up and taken to a custom-built shelf in a walk-in safe in the corner of the room. When the last employee exited the safe, the latch was thrown and the combination dial was spun.

Parsuitt recalled that "Rangers had once raided the Balinese Room 62 nights in a row, without a single bust." With such regularity, the lawmen were incorporated into the entertainment of the evening. As the band struck up the University of Texas marching song, "The Eyes of Texas Are Upon You," the conductor, gesturing toward the door, announced, "Ladies and Gentleman, I now present the Texas Rangers!" as the first ten-gallon white hats burst through the door. Parsuitt admitted that "it was just an act anyway because even the Rangers were getting money under the table."

Members of a committee of Texas legislators, headed by Estes Kefauver, subpoenaed amiable Sheriff Frank L. Biaggne, who served from 1933 to 1957, to testify on the floor of the House. When asked why he didn't close down the Balinese, the "good ol' boy" tugged at his hat and stammered, "Ah, shucks. I'm not a member—I can't get in."

THE MOTHER OF ALL RAIDS THAT NEVER HAPPENED

Up in Austin, Attorney General Will Wilson, the "AG Who Would Be Governor," needed the "hook" as a strong law and order reformer to advance politically. He and his staff set up an elaborate sting operation to cross the Causeway to march on Galveston Island, much like Julius Caesar's march on Rome in 49 BC to end that empire. The first reconnaissance took seven months and cost "way over $3,000 in state funds" to compile a hit list of raid targets and then a stakeout. On the eve of June 5, 1957, a task force of more than one hundred Texas law enforcers, armed with secret search warrants, waited with an entourage of handpicked photographers and reporters to invade Galveston Island and catch illegal gamblers in the act. However, when none of the targeted clubs was open that evening, the "Mother of All Raids" was canceled.

Five days later, the law prevailed as the Attorney General's Office sought injunctions against fifty-two clubs at Galveston's 56th District Court. Led by crime crusader-editor Clyde Ragsdale of the obscure, small-town *Texas City Sun*, photographs of Rangers relentlessly smashing illegal slots and gaming equipment made the national news. As publicity grew, Wilson was forced to issue felony gambling charges. By the end of June 1957, his injunctions had ended all bets on Galveston Island; the Maceo empire fell. In addition, Wilson never made it to the Texas Governor's Mansion. He was later implicated in the notorious Sharpstown banking scandal and ended up with a twenty-year jail sentence.

As for the Maceos? Across the street from the Balinese, Sam called the glamorous penthouse suite of the Hotel Galvez home. After his first childless marriage ended, he married dancer/Hollywood starlet Edna Sedgwick, and they started their family at the Buccaneer Hotel two blocks to the west. Twin boys were born, followed by a daughter.

During the late '40s, Edna convinced him to build a home in Galveston's "Garden Spot," Cedar Lawn. He bought four lots and hired Frank Sinatra's Palm Springs architects, Williams, Williams and Williams, to design a California Contemporary, completed in 1951. Unfortunately, that same year, Sam died of cancer in surgery at John Hopkins at the age of fifty-seven and never lived there. Three years later, his widow sold it and moved to New Orleans. Also in 1954, older brother Papa Rose, who supplied the muscle for the syndicate, died of heart failure at the age of sixty-six.

All of their descendants became honest, hardworking, middle-class Galveston citizens, working to save lives on the Beach Patrol, hotel management or peddling spices and their famous muffulettas at a deli. The big-name Hollywood entertainers and rich high rollers, with their wives and mistresses, who had once "played the Island" along with the Maceos' pit bosses, dealers, suppliers and henchmen went west to Vegas or the coast. All the other colorful characters during its wide-open "Free State" days faded into fond memories of this Galveston that was.

THE GALS OF GALVESTON

Infamous Postoffice Street

Prostitution was nothing new to the port city of Galveston, Texas, when young Mathilda "Mollie" Walters came to the Island from New Orleans in 1868. Indeed, an identifiable red-light district had clearly been established north of Broadway, just west of 25th Street. When the occupation of Federal troops after the Civil War added to the usual seamen and traveling salesmen who frequented downtown, the young madam opened her first bordello on 25th Street between Market and Mechanic. Arrested for "keeping a disorderly house" in 1870, Miss Mollie pleaded guilty, paid her fine of $100 and then returned to business as usual.

Although her original brick house became a landmark, the heart of the segregated district was Postoffice Street, or Avenue E. During the prosperous

1880s, Mollie Walters invested in the area, buying several parcels of land. Strategically, she chose the northwest corner of Postoffice at 26th Street on which to build her two-story, custom-frame "female boarding house," with entrances on both streets and the alley. The house extended a full half block on 26th Street to the alley to accommodate the long central hall upstairs, lined with door after door into bedrooms. The latticework on the front porch offered discreet clients anonymity.

By this time, Galveston was the second-largest port in the United States, with as many as thirty ships in port every day. In 1897, the federal government again contributed to the growth of carnal commerce when it established a coastal artillery installation at Fort Crockett. Thanks to medical students and a growing group of conventioneers, Postoffice Street flourished. Referred to as "the Line," it was soon lined with brightly lit bordellos. Clients who walked the street looking for company were said to be going "Down the Line," according to Mary Remmers, from one house to the next.

In quality, Miss Mollie's bordello was top of the line, offering the wealthiest clients all the decadence the era had to offer. Ushered into the downstairs parlor, the men listened to live music as they met and mingled with elegantly dressed courtesans, until the client made his choice. A maid manager guarded the stairs as she took care of business. The amount of time was decided and the fee paid—usually $10 for fifteen minutes. The working girl was given a towel, and the two disappeared up the stairs. If the client took longer, the maid collected more cash, often interrupting with a knock on the door. To spend the whole night with one of Mollie's courtesans cost $300.

Towels served as the bordello's accounting system—at the end of the evening, the number of towels turned in had to match the number of paying customers the maid had recorded in the ledger. One twelve-year-old towel girl couldn't figure out what they were doing with all those towels every night.

The prices on the Line reflected the overall quality of the house's décor, the ladies themselves and the number of available amenities. Less opulent houses charged between one and five dollars. The working-class sailors and soldiers were relegated to the older girls at Mollie's backdoor.

Although the number of girls had dwindled to three, the sixty-seven-year-old Walters continued to run the business until she retired in 1906. She then leased the house to Corinne Pearce for $100 per month, and Miss Mollie bought a home out of the district at 3518 Avenue O, where she quietly passed away on December 14, 1908. Pearce renamed the bordello The Club. During her tenure as madam, she had a run-in

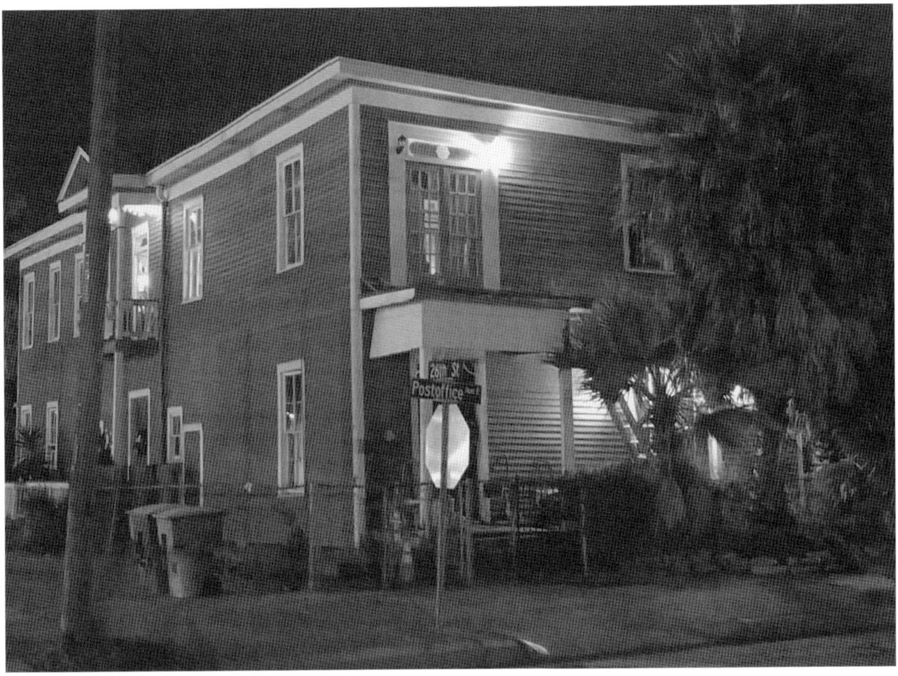

"Molly" Walter's Bordello, 26th and Postoffice. *Courtesy of James Anderson.*

with a john who met an untimely demise. Tried for murder, she was acquitted.

Maintaining the quality established by Mollie Walters, Hazel Harvey took over the bordello on the corner of 26th and Postoffice in 1918. Known as "Mother" Harvey because she took such good care of all the boys, she employed only high-class courtesans, some with legitimate careers. Busiest during Prohibition, Mother Harvey's encouraged clients to imbibe in bootleg brew, while her ladies were only allowed to drink watered-down whiskey.

In 1944, the old Mollie Walters place passed into the hands of Mary R., who, since she had one bad eye, was known as Gouch-Eye. During her tenure, her top-of-the-line house became part of a statewide syndicate. At some point, screened doors were added to the upstairs bedrooms to allow clients to view the choices. When business was slow, her girls took turns working the windows, dressed respectfully in shorts and blouses. Old Gouch-Eye left the business before Texas attorney general Will Wilson "closed down Galveston" in 1957. It seems she saw it coming in the Houston newspapers.

Sir, You Got to Treat, Trade or Travel

Still standing in tribute to Galveston's infamous red-light district, 2528 Postoffice is the lone survivor of the era when men walked the streets and women called the shots to keep their customers satisfied. The madams' mantra was "Sir, you got to treat, trade or travel."

In the business of carnal commerce, they were upper management—landladies who received 40 percent of the courtesans' fees and also charged them rent. In exchange, the house paid attorney fees, doctor bills and bribes to law enforcement, if needed. Town talk about the madams ran rampant, and oh the colorful tales it told! With historical facts sketchy and memories unpredictable at best, these legends took on the guise of truth.

As a rule, the madams served their apprenticeship as working girls before retiring as entrepreneurs in this female-run business. Although they no longer worked the evening shift, they would entertain special guests in their private suites occasionally. As a result, several married prominent Island citizens and moved legitimately into Galveston society. One even provided the capital for her merchant husband's successful business.

Queen Laura fancied her house an exclusive county club during the not-so-gay 1890s. Making regular business trips into the city with her coach and footman, she frequented the beach racetrack to promote her business among sport-loving Galvestonians. Fondly remembered for her flowing, floor-length black hair, Queen Laura reigned regally until she retired to New Orleans, a wealthy woman.

One madam during Prohibition was Lula W. She married a short Frenchman with curly black hair to blend with her beautiful auburn hair. This self-appointed "Mayor of Postoffice Street," an usher who passed the collection plate in church every Sunday, presided over holiday dinners at 1702 with his relatives and Lula's girls—just one big happy family. While the rest of the country suffered during the Great Depression, little was repressed on Galveston Island.

On par with Mother Harvey's top-of-the-line house was Mary Russell's bordello. She recruited well-bred college coeds to work the summer trade. In turn, the girls earned their fall tuition. One of her recruits, the daughter of a prominent Houstonian, worked her summer vacation just for fun—and a little pocket money.

Russell's house and contents could be "bought out" for an entire evening. On one occasion, the madam sequestered a twelve-year-old errand boy on behalf of her clients. Approaching one of these gentlemen, he pleaded that his boss was expecting him back at the store, but rather than releasing the youngster, the client phoned the shopkeeper. After gorging on ice cream and soda until midnight, the boy again approached the gentleman, this time citing his mother's house rules. The gentleman let him go home after tipping him a ten-dollar bill to make up for his lost hourly wage of sixty cents. Months later, the errand boy was sent to his office. When the gentleman asked, "Haven't I seen you somewhere before?" the youngster reminded him about that night at Madam Mary's bordello.

Perhaps this gentleman was John Sealy Jr., as a bordello was his favorite hangout. This successful oilman never married but took over the house periodically to party for two or three days at a stretch. Other famous clients included politicians. Galveston's Mayor Herbert Y. Cartwright swore that an up-and-comer named L.B. Johnson "used to like to get lost for a while" among the Postoffice Street bordellos, as did Governor Shiver, who would "disappear for a few days," according to author Gary Cartwright.

Granville Price's Thesis

One of Galveston's more colorful madams on Postoffice Street was Tiger Lil. A beautiful woman with porcelain skin like a "china doll," she wore the first see-through blouse on the Island with a tiger-striped leotard, probably during the 1940s. After her bordello was raided one night, she drove her big black car to the local Sherwin-Williams paint store, determined to give her bordello a new look. Paying cash, she bought three gallons of paint: fiesta orange, holiday turquoise and flame red. This combination created a sharp contrast to the typical drab, green-shuttered houses in the district—just like the madam herself. Legend has it that Tiger Lil married her pimp. When he proved unfaithful, she shot him, ending her flashy life in prison gray.

While Tiger Lil was just a memory, sketchy and unpredictable at best, Granville Price's master's thesis, "A Sociological Study of a Segregated District," documented in detail the lives of several madams during the Roaring Twenties. His profiles of prostitutes ranged from the story of Mary and Violet, "the two hags"—small-town Texas girls who had been seduced into the business—to Alice, the "beer lady" who profited from not one but two vice businesses on Galveston Island.

Born on a Michigan farm in 1904, she'd married a man who deserted her after she gave birth to his baby. With only one "skill," the beautiful and intelligent Alice was kept in comparative luxury until she decided to move south in pursuit of a more secure means to support her child, who stayed back on the farm. By 1926, she had become the star of Postoffice Street, demanding and receiving special consideration from madams in exchange for access to her exclusive clientele. One of them, bootlegger Tony Cuicci, bankrolled her own business venture: a "beer flat," where she became the profitable hostess until she drank herself out of business.

Mrs. Ardis Smith (or Smythe) ran a neat little brick house on infamous Postoffice with a certain dignity and aloofness. "The only remaining madam who radiated any glamour," this philosophical proprietress protected the privacy of her upscale clients.

In awe of her petty criminal father, May Bell Ash left her home in the Dallas slums during the summer of 1929 at the legal age of twenty-one. Working the leading hotels in Texas and Oklahoma, she came to the Island frequently and had no fear of prosecution. Although she originally wanted to go into aviation, she decided to write her "message for people who were troubled about sexual problems" after reading a great deal. An acute observer of human nature, she told many tales about the perversities of her patrons—just which she delighted in, the telling or the doing, wasn't clear.

Janice came to Galveston during World War I from her Philadelphia home, the daughter of French parents. She established her own house in 1927, working constantly during the evening shift as madam of the only "French" house in the district: Ooh, La Laa! Vigorous and active, she claimed to be forty years old in 1929, even though her lumpy figure, wrinkled face and straggly hair declared her older—as did the presence of a nineteen-year-old son.

Author Granville Price worked on the editorial staff of the *Galveston Daily News* as the police and court reporter, which allowed him access to all kinds of inside information. His thoroughly researched thesis, based on actual interviews at the time, earned him a Master of Arts degree from the University of Texas–Austin. It reached a logical, but not necessarily moral, conclusion: carnal commerce was a major contributor to the Galveston economy. Why? Certain elements within its population created a demand for the world's oldest profession that kept the madams chanting their mantra—"Sir, you gotta treat, trade or travel."

First, seamen and dock laborers of every nationality spent several days at a stretch in the second-largest port in the world, where usually fifteen to thirty ships docked any given day. Paid in cash, these crews were directed to the district, which was within walking distance.

In addition, the U.S. Army stationed at Fort Crockett, along with the Third Attack Group of Aviation Corps, supplied an additional five hundred to eight hundred potential clients. Medical students at the University of Texas Medical Branch were predominantly male, as were conventioneers. Combining a basic law of nature with a larger proportion of men to women simply set up a basic law of business: the men demanded a service and the ladies supplied. Using Price's numbers, author Gary Cartwright estimated that the ratio of prostitutes to young, unmarried males was 1:55, ranking Galveston Island a world-class city in this commodity. You do the numbers.

Another advantage was present: during an eight-year period, police did not record a single rape in the city of Galveston.

THE OFFICIAL "SPIN"

Galveston's principal economic base was commerce, not industry. Carnal commerce was a valuable commodity in a port city where lusty seamen were eager to spend their hard-earned cash on the simple pleasures of life. Like gambling and drinking, prostitution was considered a natural part of Island culture—aka the "Free State of Galveston." With that rationalization, the local authorities maintained a "laissez-faire attitude toward vice" throughout the history of infamous Postoffice Street.

Indeed, the only "natural" law that was consistently enforced by local authorities over the years was intercourse between white and black citizens. In 1925, a miscegenation ordinance went into effect that prohibited biracial sex. The houses were segregated by race. According to Ray Miller, "miscegenation and murder were about the only activities the police concerned themselves with."

However, on several occasions, authorities from off the Island intervened. In August 1917, the War Department passed a national law that banned houses of prostitution within five miles of a military base. This officially closed Galveston's bordellos, but the girls were allowed to stay.

Mere law, of course, did not stop sex, so the next year, the Feds complained that the Island city was the worst in Texas for venereal disease. In order to keep the military camps in the area, the Texas legislature passed a state law in 1918 that mandated a free clinic to offer curative measures for gonorrhea and syphilis at no cost to the girls. After World War I, it was business as usual on Postoffice Street.

"Every city that has tried to repress prostitution has found that it's impossible," said Jack E. Pearce, who was elected mayor in 1925. He served for the next ten years during the "boosterism" of Galveston Island as the greatest resort in the Southwest. "In the segregated district," he stated, "they do the least harm to the population of the city, and the police know where they are in case something happens." All working girls in the world's oldest profession were required to stay in the segregated district to ply their trade, as local authorities agreed that it was realistic to expect prostitution in a seaport—it was merely a question of management.

In 1936, city officials mandated that all prostitutes receive biweekly medical examinations, certified with health cards. Every woman working in carnal commerce received a health card that included fingerprints, mug shots, health records, drug tests and VD inspections. If all was well, the doctor issued a clean bill of health, and the card had to be displayed in the women's rooms at the bordello. Some of Galveston's finest actually escorted the ladies to the clinic every two weeks.

Periodically, the police raided to check these health cards. However, fines for noncompliance were nominal, and "raids" were announced in advance. Those girls who had contracted a venereal disease went to a free clinic behind the police station at 20th and Mechanic for treatment. Willie Burns, chief of police from 1933 to 1957, remembered that they were given some kind of brown liquid to drink. He also noted that the houses on Postoffice Street were clean and "everyone behaved themselves," as the district was patrolled by policemen on foot, including Burns' father, who had walked that beat previously. By the way, Willie's brother-in-law was Frank Biaggne, the Galveston County sheriff who couldn't raid the Balinese room for illegal gambling because he wasn't a member.

The man closest to God on Galveston Island, Bishop Christopher Byrne, was in favor of Postoffice Street, even though he did campaign against community bathing, the sale of condoms and for the abolition of the Pageant of Pulchritude on a regular basis. In his master's thesis, Granville Price described the bishop as a "tall, scholarly…crusading" clergyman with an Irish brogue, a man who observed that "as long as man has free will, some of us will fall into impurity…due to man's innate sin and weakness."

With the advent of World War II, once again the U.S. War Department warned Galveston that "commercial prostitution is a detriment to national defense" and ordered local officials to shut down bordellos. Under pressure, the city commission declared the red-light district closed in 1941 for the duration of the war. This did not end prostitution but merely sent it underground. As one madam stated, "You could always get in the back door."

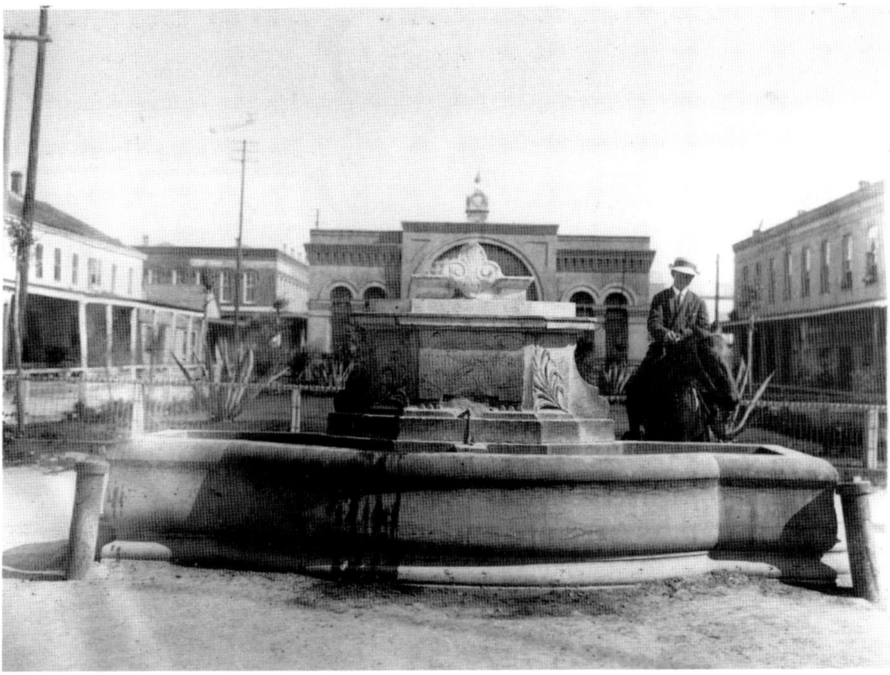

One of seventeen "Rosenberg Fountains for Both Men and Beasts" located at 20th and Mechanic Streets. It now sits at 21st and Postoffice. *Courtesy of the Rosenberg Library, Galveston, Texas.*

One year later, an estimated eight hundred professionals and countless amateur "victory girls," scattered throughout the city, offering their services to servicemen. Although the military issued condoms to recruits, John Sealy Hospital opened a VD clinic when penicillin became available in May 1944. After the war, the madams reestablished business as usual in the segregated district of Postoffice Street.

A prominent City Father of the Jewish faith, Isaac "Ike" Kempner, characterized prostitution as "the most ancient and agreeable of all professions." Financer of the grade raising E.R. Cheeseborough and Jacob Singer, city commissioner of finance and revenue, fondly recalled a huge two-story house on Broadway that was set back among the trees, behind a high fence.

The world's oldest profession prospered on Galveston Island, with only minor interference by the local authorities. One of Mother Harvey's boys, Herbert Y. Cartwright, became mayor in 1947. As a student at Ball High School in the '30s, he had hung out at her bordello, listening to the jukebox and sipping home brew. Considering it a duty and a privilege to maintain the "segregated district during his administration," Cartwright is quoted as saying, "If God couldn't stop prostitution, why should I?" to the Texas legislative committee in Austin in 1951 "in an effort to keep the 'Gals in Galveston.'"

The following mayor, George Roy Clough, pronounced prostitution a biological necessity for a seaport and then capitalized on this vice. He mandated monthly police raids on the Postoffice Street bordellos to collect fines. In a working agreement he had with the madams, the city made about an extra $1,000 per month. When questioned about the Texas Ranger citywide raid in 1957, he danced a little side step by stating that he had nothing to do with the shutdown as he "neither supported nor opposed it."

Just as with the 1900 Storm, this moral maelstrom changed the course of Galveston's history forever, capitalizing on the fact that there was just no money in morals.

UNDERSUNG HEROES AND HEROINES

Norris Wright Cuney: A Shining Light for His Race

Considered by many to be the most important black leader in nineteenth-century Texas, Norris Wright was born on the Sunnyside cotton plantation in Waller County in the Brazos River valley on May 12, 1846. The son of Colonel Philip Minor Cuney, one of the largest landowners and slaveholders in the state, and his slave Adeline Stuart, Norris Wright was the fourth of eight children. Unlike others, however, his multiracial birth—that mixed African, European and Native American ancestry—gave him a more Mediterranean appearance.

Although born slaves, the predominantly white Cuney/Stuart progeny were freed by their father before the Civil War started. Norris chose to adopt his father's surname. At his mother's insistence, he learned to play the bass violin as part of his early education before attending his father's choice, George B. Vashon's Wylies School for Blacks in Pittsburgh, Pennsylvania. Unfortunately, the beginning of the Civil War halted his college plans to attend the desegregated, coeducational Oberlin College in Ohio.

Instead, Norris Wright worked a steamship, traveling the Mississippi and Ohio Rivers. He chose, however, to spend much of his time in New Orleans, where he fell under the influence of P.B.S. Pinchback. Also educated in the North, Pinchback returned to the South after the war and was elected as the first Republican lieutenant governor of Louisiana, a precursor to the state's governorship.

Returning to Galveston at the end of the Civil War, Cuney took full advantage of being the mixed-race son of a powerful, wealthy local white politician. His mother and brothers soon joined him, living within a few blocks of one another while he began a self-study of the law and literature.

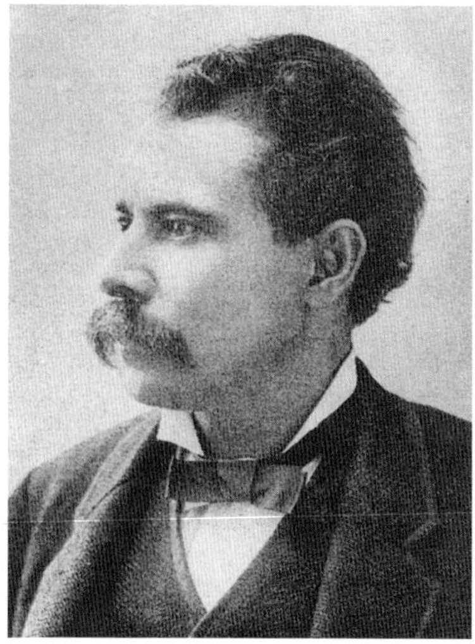

Norris Wright Cuney. *Courtesy of the Rosenberg Library, Galveston, Texas.*

By then, the city had become the state headquarters of the Freedmen's Bureau, the federal agency responsible for providing aid to former slaves to transition to a free market labor society, under the leadership of George T. Ruby. Norris Wright was also secretly involved in the Union League, a political organization focused on recruiting Freedmen to the Republican Party.

Cuney befriended Republican governor Edmund J. Davis and was named as a state delegate of the party two years later, a position he maintained for two decades. Building much political capital, he was thoroughly ingratiated within the Union League by 1870.

Turning his interests to the education of black citizens, Norris Wright worked to ensure that people of color would receive equal educational opportunities. After the Texas legislature established the public school system in 1871, he guaranteed tax allocations, as one of Galveston County's school directors, to fund schools for black students in a segregated public school system established by the biracial Reconstruction-era legislature.

Also that year, Cuney was asked to lead the Galveston chapter of the Union League when Ruby left Texas politics to be appointed as the first sergeant-at-arms of the Texas legislature. The following year, Norris Wright was appointed the federal inspector of customs for the Port of Galveston and revenue inspector at Sabine Pass.

A popular figure in the community, Cuney garnered respect from its business leaders—in particular the Galveston Cotton Exchange, which asked him to participate in promoting port improvements. During that time, he became the secretary of the Republican State Executive Committee and presided over the black Texas convention in Brenham.

On July 5, 1871, he married a local schoolteacher, Adelina Dowdie. The daughter of a mulatto slave and her white planter owner, she bore him a daughter, Maud Cuney, on February 16, 1874, and a son, Lloyd Garrison Cuney, who became an official in the Congregational Church. Maud graduated from the New England Conservatory of Music in 1895 and taught music until she married William P. Hare on August 10, 1904. Settling in Boston, Mrs. Hare became an acclaimed African folklorist and music historian, the first to champion Creole music. Her most highly regarded work was *Negro Musicians and Their Music*, published in 1936.

Their father's faith was more political, however. Norris Wright joined the Prince Hall Lodge of the Freemasons and championed its cause to be recognized in the South. In 1875, he was elected grand master of the Grand Lodge of Texas by black Masons.

After the official end of Reconstruction in 1882 with the withdrawal of federal troops, Cuney was elected alderman of the Twelfth District on the Galveston City Council the following year. He also became the special inspector for customs at the port.

Opening a stevedore company that employed five hundred black dockworkers, Norris Wright also organized a labor union, the Colored Screwmen's Benevolent Association, in 1883. Although the white union controlled the docks, he encouraged his workers into open competition, crossing white picket lines and accepting lower pay to increase their presence of black workers at the port. As a result, his company secured the stevedoring contract with Galveston's largest cotton shipper, the Morgan Lines. The years 1884–96 became known as the "Cuney Era."

Norris Wright Cuney died in San Antonio on March 4, 1898. Harmony Hall at 22nd and Church was packed with three thousand black and white mourners, with another one thousand waiting outside. His funeral procession, led by the Galveston Brass Band, included Screwmen's associates, black longshoremen and representatives of Masonic Lodges, Odd Fellows and Knights of Pythias. They marched from the Hall to Reedy Chapel AME on Broadway between 20th and 21st, where pastor Reverend Moody eulogized him as a "Manly Man," a "shining light for his race" who evened the odds between the races. Cuney was buried at Lakeview Cemetery on 57th Street.

Most of our knowledge of this "undersung" African American hero comes from his biography, *Norris Wright Cuney: A Tribune of the Black People*, written by his daughter, Maud Hare, in 1913. She died in Boston on February 13, 1936, but was buried on Galveston Island at Lakeview Cemetery, next to her parents.

Rosenberg Library's Frank Chauncey Patten: Quintessential Head Librarian

Galveston's biggest benefactor, Henry Rosenberg, bequeathed the bulk of his estate to the founding of a "free, public library." To ensure its success, he included an ongoing endowment fund and governing structure. Although not established until eleven years after his death, the Rosenberg Library Association strictly adhered to those provisions in his will by establishing a board of twenty trustees, appointed for unpaid life terms, who would preside over a head librarian who managed day-to-day activities. The first CEO of that nonprofit organization was not just suited to that position—he acutely manifested its benefactor's vision for the library to serve as the cultural center of intellectual growth on the Island.

Frank Chauncey Patten was born on June 15, 1855, in Rochester, New York, to British parents Horace and Olive Maria (Rice) Patten. Following Benjamin Hall of the Adventist movement, they eventually settled on a farm in Oshkosh, Wisconsin, in 1874. Here, son Frank attended and graduated from the state normal school, teaching there intermittently until 1881.

During Frank's tenure, he walked the 1,750 miles to Texas at age twenty-four, making his way as a handyman in exchange for room and board. On Galveston Island, he lived in a hut he'd built from driftwood on the San Luis Peninsula and ended up in Brazoria County, where he earned his teacher's certificate. He established a school for African American children at Live Oak Point and taught there until its funding ran out in January 1880.

He returned to Wisconsin and attended Ripon College. Working as a student library assistant, Patten discovered his true calling and graduated from the first class of the Columbia College School of Library Economy. Led by Melville Dewey, who had invented the Dewey decimal system used for years to catalogue books, the two men formed a professional bond that lasted throughout Patten's career.

As a public librarian, Patten worked for seven years at Helena, Montana, before he moved on to the Lenox Library in New York City in the same capacity. But the position he really desired was head librarian, "where there is opportunity to work out plans for personal helpfulness to the common people, and especially the young."

On July 10, 1900, the State of Texas granted a charter to the Rosenberg Library Association of Galveston. Using Dewey as a reference, Frank C. Patten applied for and was appointed as the new library's executive director three years later. His first task was to supervise the completion of the building itself. Part of his influence can be noted in the spacious, comfortable and homey reading/study areas, with many quiet nooks for patrons.

The head librarian set the structure's dedication on what would have been Henry Rosenberg's eightieth birthday, June 22, 1904, in honor of its benefactor. Amid much pomp and circumstance, Patten spoke about the new library as "a place of great activity, serving all classes of people with all sorts of needs...extending its... energies in all directions." After that initial opening, he moved the annual Henry Rosenberg Day to May 1.

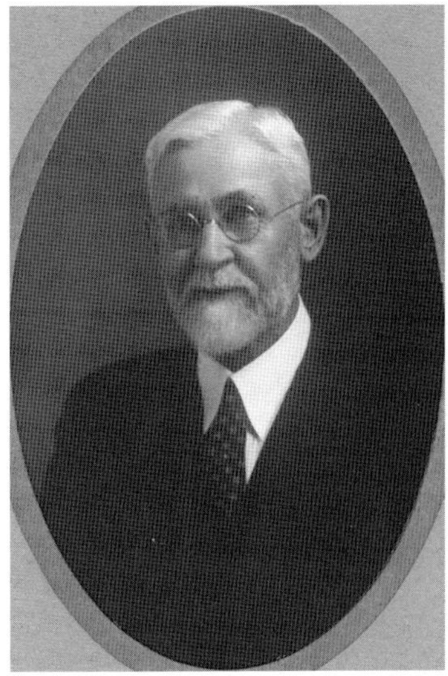

Frank Chauncey Patten. *Courtesy of the Rosenberg Library, Galveston, Texas.*

Frank C. also established a firm foundation on which future head librarians could build. Realizing Rosenberg's vision of the library as the center of intellectual growth and moral development on the Island, he then methodically developed a capable, efficient and competent staff, including a separate children's department headed by its own librarian.

Almost immediately, a racial controversy arose when African Americans were excluded from the free public library. That influential group, strengthened by the political power of Norris Wright Cuney, petitioned the Texas legislature and was granted an additional appropriation of $4,000 to build a library of its own. Constructed adjoining Central High School at 27th and Avenue M, the Colored Branch of the Rosenberg Library opened in January 1905. Its full-time African American staff was led by J.R. Gibson and included Jesse MacGuire Dent acting as dean of women.

During the next ten years, Frank C. Patten turned his attention to the acquisition of books and research materials on a wide range of subjects, from literature to history, arts and sciences. In addition, he mandated a system of fines for any damage done to its growing book collection.

To establish the library as *the* repository of all Galveston and Texas ephemera, one anecdote recounts how Patten and trustee John M. Winterbotham went from house to house, person to person, gathering large stacks of valuable historic manuscripts, journals, records, letters and memorabilia, including the papers of Samuel May Williams, the Bordens and the Galveston City Company, among others. This demanded more storage space, so the building was enlarged by 1914. Patten also implemented a popular public lecture series on a variety of subjects by respected and knowledgeable speakers to support Rosenberg's vision of his library as a cultural center.

A man of many talents but only one passion, the quintessential head librarian and lifelong bachelor published a biography of his benefactor's life and library in 1918, *Henry Rosenberg, 1824–1893*. Serving in his post until the end, Frank Patten passed into eternity himself on January 6, 1934. He left most of his own estate to the Rosenberg Library, Galveston, Texas. The year after his death, the *Dallas Journal* estimated his contribution to have been $38,000.

In addition, the first head librarian—one of only ten in the history of Galveston's public library—left his own ephemera file, which included the published history of his family, a ceremonial Knights Templar sword, a 32nd degree certificate dated 1914 and his personal correspondences that included a note from the Seaside Hotel on the northwest corner of Tremont and Avenue Q that was destroyed by fire in December 1917—all of which are now accessible to the public.

"MADAME" OLGA SAMAROFF

Madame Olga Samaroff was a celebrated concert pianist, author, music critic and teacher who spent her formative years in Galveston. In San Antonio, Texas, she was born Lucy Mary Agnes Hickenlooper on August 8, 1880. Her father, Carlos Hickenlooper, was stationed at Fort Sam Houston. After he resigned his army commission, he settled the family on the Island at 24th and Avenue M, abandoning them after the 1900 Storm washed away his business.

Lucy was left in the very capable of hands of her mother, Jane Loening Hickenlooper, and grandmother Lucy (Palmer) Loening Grunewald, both famous concert pianists in their own right. Her education was completed at the Ursuline convent just a block and a half away.

Her inherited musical talent became apparent by the age of ten, and with no maestros stateside, she moved to Paris in 1894 with Grandmother Grunewald, where she won a scholarship to its conservatoire. The first American young lady to receive such an honor, she studied under Élie-

Miriam Delaborde and Antoine François Marmontel. Graduating three years later, she moved to Berlin to work with Russian pianist-teacher Ernest Hutcheson. In addition, Lucy also studied with Constantin von Sternberg and Ernst Jedliczka, a former student of Tchaikovsky's.

Amid the many protestations by her guardians, Lucy met and married Russian engineer Boris Loutsky there. The young couple moved to St. Petersburg, where Lucy broadened her musical boundaries by staying away from the piano. When her husband revealed his cruelty toward her, she divorced him and began focusing on her future as a concert pianist.

Her talent already recognized in Europe, Lucy Hickenlooper Loutsky moved back to the United States, where she engaged an enterprising agent. His first suggestion was that she change her name to sound *less* American. After 1904, she would be known only as Olga Samaroff (pronounced "sa-*mar*-off") in honor of her grandmother's Russian heritage.

To complete her makeover, she orchestrated her own concert debut with money she borrowed from a wealthy relative in Cincinnati, again going against the will of her protectors. On January 18, 1905, she appeared at Carnegie Hall under the baton of Walter Damrosch and the New York Symphony Orchestra. Her performance of Tchaikovsky's *Piano Concerto No. 1*, noted by critics for its "tonal color, warmth, and intellectual control," launched her career in the United States.

Suffering a severe illness in 1910, she took time out from touring, but not music. By now considered a virtuoso, Olga discovered church organist Leopold Stokowski at St. Bartholemew's in New York and promoted his career. When he debuted in Paris with the Colonne Orchestra on May 12, 1909, she played the *Concerto No. 1*. Their musical passions led to a secret marriage in 1911. She used her influence to land him the conductor's post at the Philadelphia Orchestra the following year. A daughter named Sonia was born to them in 1921, but his numerous infidelities led to divorce two years later. Samaroff kept his last name until her death and never married again.

Throughout her career, she returned to her adopted hometown to perform many times. On March 2, 1915, she played a concert at the Scottish Rite Cathedral. She also performed for the Girls' Musical Club, which her mother and grandmother had established in 1892. On November 30, 1924, an article in the *Galveston Daily News* referred to Olga as a Galvestonian who "made American Womanhood distinguished" to promote one of her many concerts held at the City Auditorium. It also noted that Thos. Goggan and Bro. was selling tickets to her recital "with spoken program notes."

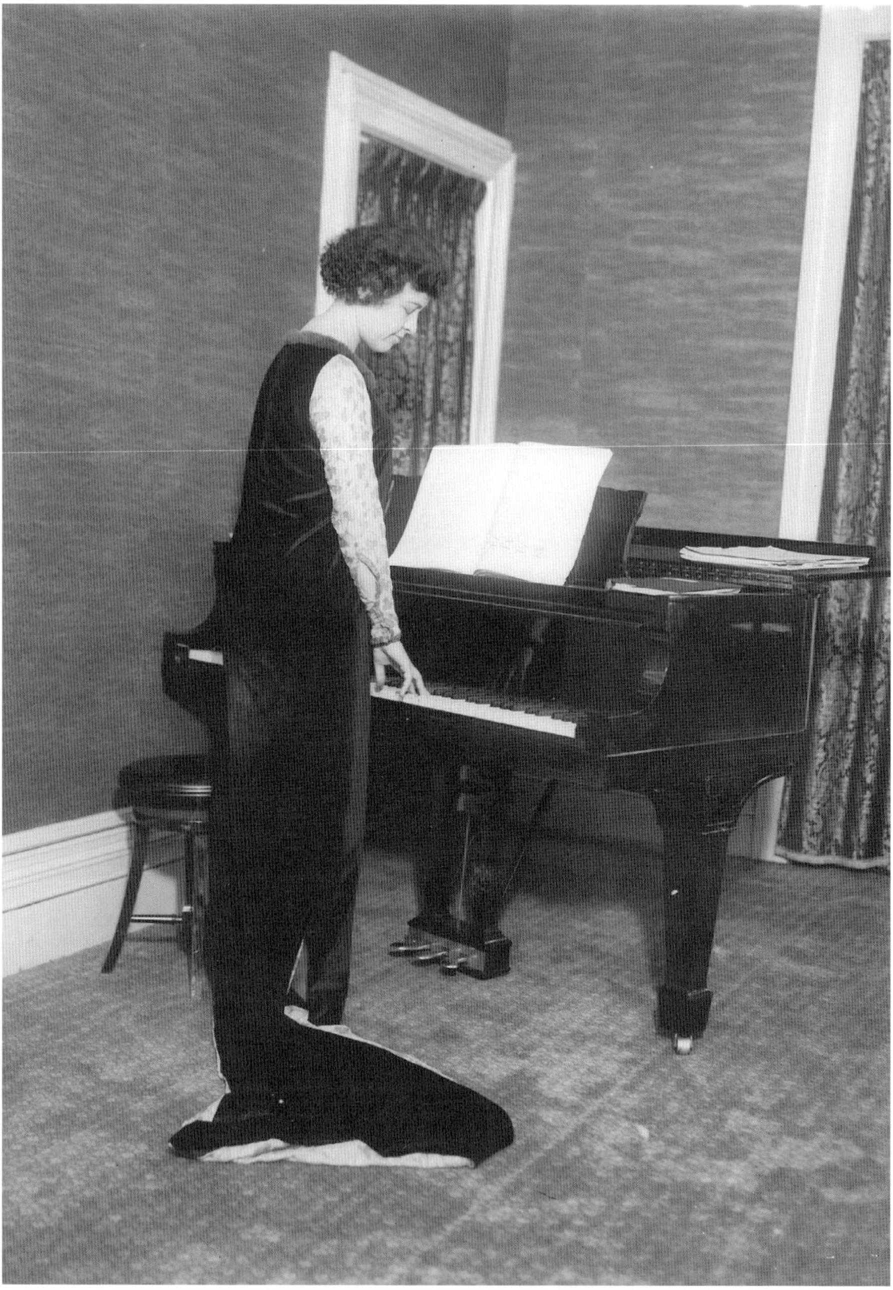

Olga Samaroff (née Lucy Mary Agnes Hickenlooper). *Author's collection.*

In 1925, she fell in her New York apartment and injured her shoulder, forcing her to retire from performing. Turning to teaching, she accepted a position with the new Juilliard School of Music. She also wrote for the *New York Evening Post* as a music critic and commuted to Philadelphia, where she chaired the piano department of that city's conservatory. To provide performance opportunities for her students, who affectionately called her "Madame," she organized the Schubert Memorial Foundation in 1928. Eleven years later, she penned her autobiography, *An American Musician's Story*.

Her Laymen's Music Courses followed three years after that to foster music education. Broadcast during the 1940s on NBC, Samaroff was the first music teacher on both radio and TV. During one of her radio programs, she played a Blind Auditions game: a contestant had to decide if the pianist, performing behind a partition, was male or female. "Madame" was very much amused when 92 percent incorrectly guessed a man when the player was actually one of her female students.

Headstrong, independent and an extremely gifted concert pianist, Olga Samaroff (née Lucy Hickenlooper) died of a heart attack the evening of May 17, 1948, after giving several piano lessons that day. Her body, which was not discovered until the following day, was cremated.

LOCAL LEGENDS

"Galveston Goddesses": Bathing Beauties and Beyond

Since 1910, attractive young ladies, especially those in bathing attire, have represented the face and form of Galveston Island. What better way to call attention to an event, sport or festival, than framing it with a pretty girl in a form-fitting costume of the era? Real or imagined, almost every decade had its own version of the "Galveston Goddess"—from artists' conceptions to bevies of living dolls, wearing everything from matching outfits to modest bathing suits to bikinis—with the seashore as background.

The first water nymph was Miss Galvie Stone, born from a man's imagination in February 1914. Sponsored by the Retail Merchants' Association, this "radiant maiden" stood "ankle deep in sea water, wringing out little rivulets of an abbreviated bathing skirt." Thirteen-year-old Dickinson lad Nicholas McCalab named her, while the *Galveston Daily News* chronicled her numerous adventures. Her image adorned vintage sales pieces for businesses such as the Hotel Galvez and Davidson's Dry Goods. Heralding every season, Miss Galvie Stone soon started making live appearances, portrayed by such comely naiads as Misses Frances Sedgewick and Anna Butler, assistant secretary of Galveston's Merchant's Association.

By the 1920s, however, the bloom on her cheeks had faded, and she had been replaced by the International Pageant of Pulchritude. From the

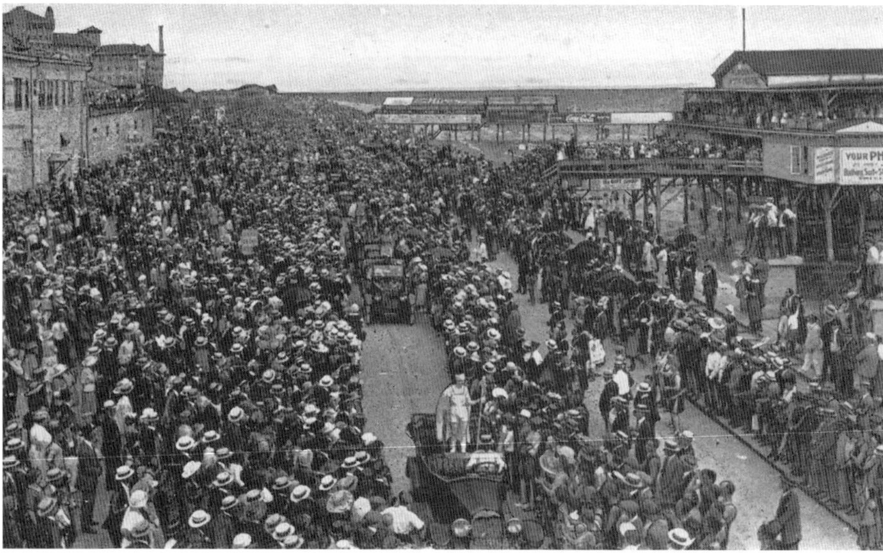

International Pageant of Pulchritude and Bathing Beauty Review. *Author's collection.*

first experiment in 1922 through 1931, this Bathing Beauty revue was *the* original international beauty contest. Representing countries from all over the world, shapely maids clad in clingy one-piece bathing suits descended on Galveston's beaches, despite objections from Catholic bishop Christopher Byrne.

Rumor had it that one of the contestants in 1931 was Dorothy Lamour, representing New Orleans; she would find future fame in the Bing Cosby/Bob Hope "Road" movies and others. Eventually, the pageant itself traveled the world, morphing into today's Miss Universe contest. A pale shadow of the original was revived several years ago as the vintage Galveston Beach Review.

During the World War II years, a more wholesome atmosphere prevailed when female quadruplets were BOI on February 1, 1939, at St. Mary's Hospital to Mr. and Mrs. W. Ellis Badgett. In exchange for a home at 926 Broadway, complete with a picture window, the baby faces of sisters Joan, Joyce, Jeraldine and Jeanette charmed their way into the national spotlight, bringing their coastal hometown with them. "Galveston's Sweethearts" served as honorary flower girls at the Alice Faye/Phil Harris Galvez wedding, celebrated birthdays and holidays, posed with Johnny "Tarzan" Weissmuller during the 1946 Splash Days and sold war bonds, all in the public eye. Upon their eighteenth birthday in 1957, the window closed, allowing the young ladies to begin their lives anew, out of the spotlight.

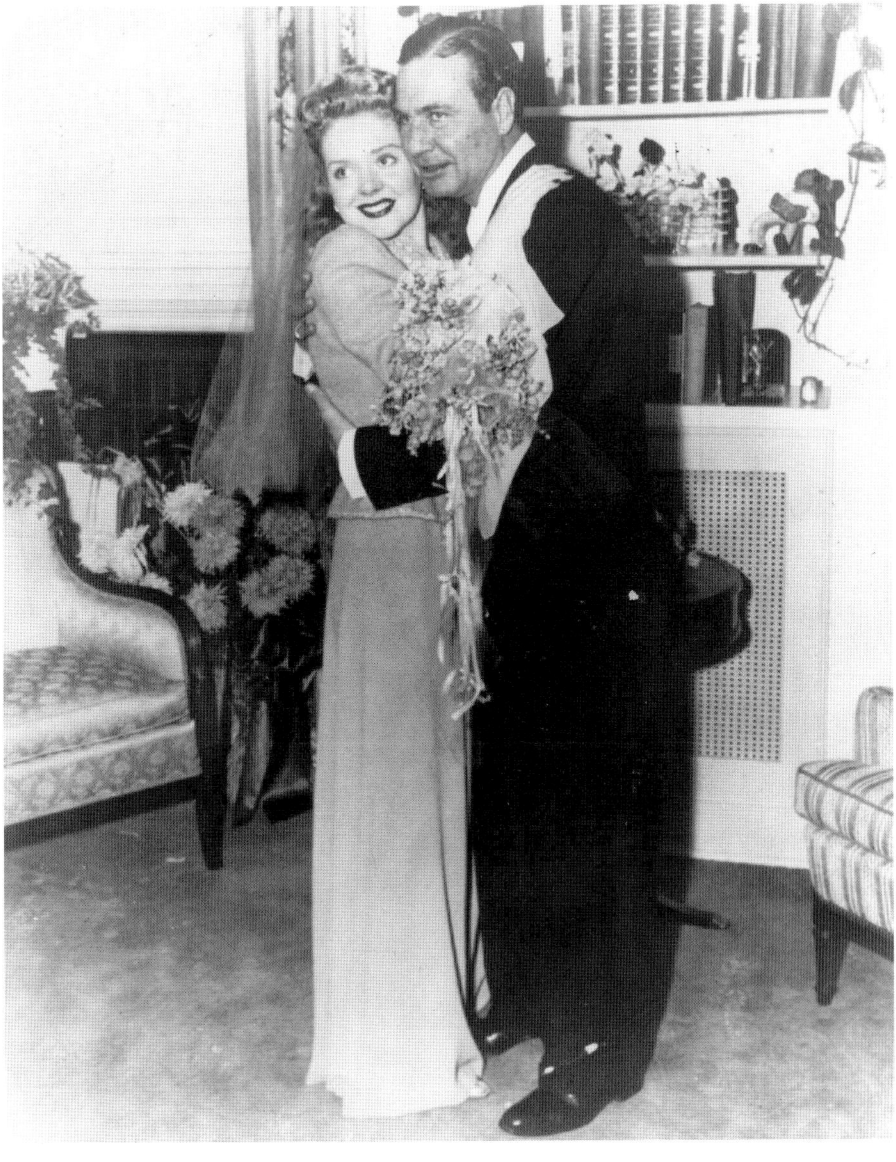

Alice Faye and Phil Harris at the wedding in September 1941 in the Maceo penthouse suite of the Hotel Galvez. *Author's collection.*

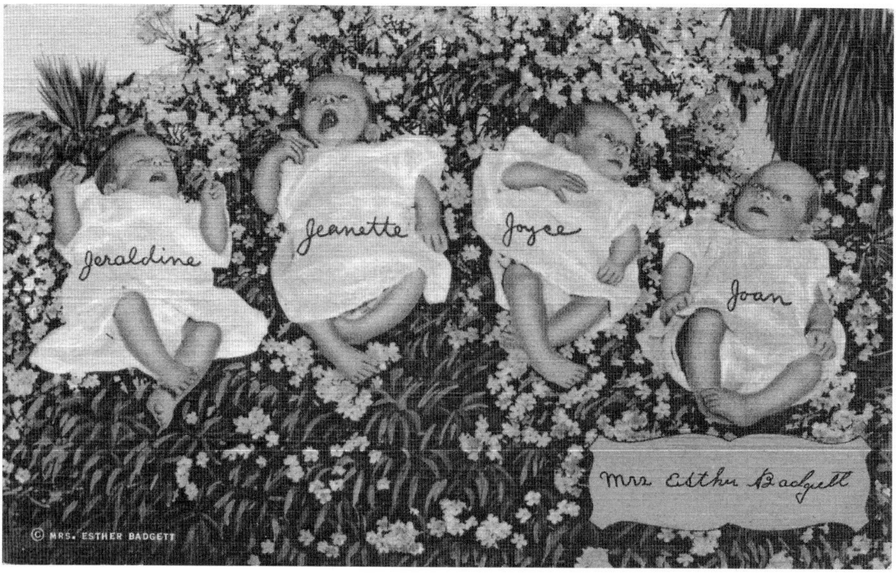

Postcard of Badgett Quadruplets, printed by mother Mrs. Esther Badgett. *Author's collection.*

Sponsored by the Galveston Junior Chamber of Commerce, the first official Miss Galveston Pageant was scheduled for June 8, 1963. However, no entries were received by May 31, so the beauty contest was canceled. That same year, a junior high student realized her childhood dream as a model for E.S. Levy. Lovely, blond Charlotte McCowan won the title of "Miss Sportscar," triumphing over Sammi Lou Williams, who later became "Miss Houston." Charli was also named "Miss KILE" when the winner made an abrupt unexpected exit.

Active in the city's junior chamber of commerce, Miss McCowan was appointed "Miss Galveston" several years later, officially becoming the city's face and form. Whenever a pretty girl in a bathing suit was needed for a photo shoot, she answered the call. Among the events she promoted were football season, outboard motorboat races and the importance of buckling up those newfangled seatbelts. Her reign ended during her senior year at Ball High School, when she was elected cheerleader and went to work at the Peacock Café to maintain that costly honor.

Online images of the next "Miss Galveston" surfaced around 1971–72. Lovely Latina Esmeralda Y'Barra, proclaimed "Miss Maritime" by Mayor Edward Schreiber on May 22, 1971, graced various media as a seductive mermaid. The following year, she participated in the Miss Shrimp Festival

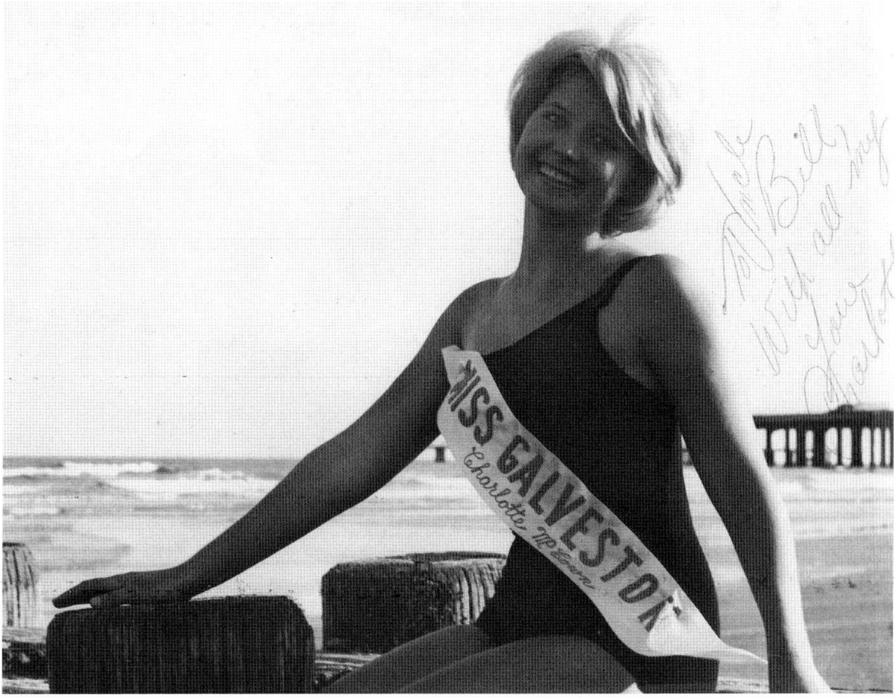

Charlotte McCowan, Miss Galveston, 1966. *Courtesy of Charlotte McCown Rohack.*

contest, representing Manuel and Yolanda Corella's restaurant as "Miss Taco." After the April 29 parade, "Ya Ya" walked away with the title.

The title "Miss Galveston" disappeared during the latter part of that decade. Other young lovelies, however, would revise the concept—sans bathing suit and seashore—when oilman George Mitchell revived Galveston's Mardi Gras to open his grand new Tremont House hotel on Ship's Mechanic Row in 1985.

Originally established in 1871, the Krewe of the Knights of Momus, an elite group of mostly Galveston men, returned to orchestrate the purple, green and gold winter Lenten festival. Their first order of business every year was a Coronation Ball of debutantes to form the Royal Court. Similar to the college-sponsored Rose Bowl court, these young ladies hailed from various Texas cities, with at least one from the Island. To prove their worthiness, the couture-clad courtiers performed the deep and awkward Texas bow on the stage of the Grand 1894 Opera House the first Saturday of the fifteen-day celebration.

Then the new Momus King Frivolous would be unmasked, pairing with his Galveston-born Queen to reign over the festivities until the day before Ash Wednesday—the official "Mardi Gras," aka "Fat Tuesday," which marked the final indulgence before the austere six-week period of penance that ended on Easter Sunday.

As for "Miss Galveston," the Galveston Chamber of Commerce attempted to again revive the beauty pageant in October 2014. A young lady was crowned on the Grand's stage and served as ambassador for the city, performing nonprofit work and making appearances, but there was not a 2015 contest. There will, however, be another Mardi Gras Court, King and Queen next winter.

Lafitte's Treasure

French nobleman, merchant seaman, pirate patriot/hero, "Terror of the Gulf" and entrepreneur—Jean Lafitte's legend is rooted in the early history of the Gulf Coast, beginning in New Orleans, moving on to Galveston and ending in an enigma. Purposefully shrouding himself in mystery with conflicting statements, this larger-than-life opportunist secured a place in Texas folklore with his final farewell, leaving behind his buried treasure on the Island; however, that treasure is merely "in the eye of the beholder."

Believed to have been born in Bayonne pre-Revolutionary France as the son of a French father and Spanish mother, Jean left as a young stowaway, seeking his fortune on the high seas. Soon, he captained his first ship complete with cargo. However, during his maiden voyage, a Spanish buccaneer attacked and took everything, including the life of his young and beautiful dark-eyed wife, scuttling his ship near St. Domingue on the isle of Hispaniola, present-day Haiti and the Dominican Republic.

Embittered and heartbroken, Lafitte sought vengeance. The letters of marque he secured from Colombia in South America allowed him to legally attack Spanish ships from his Caribbean refuge. When war broke out during the 1790s, he left, settling just off the coast of Louisiana, in the swamps at Barataria. With him as manager, his band of freebooters laid siege to slave ships, taking their human cargo and best booty back to the boss. His older brother, Pierre, owned a blacksmith shop in New Orleans that served as a front for Jean's privateer business. The legal smuggler became wealthy, powerful and famous. However, Louisiana governor Claiborne defined his operation as illegal and offered a price of $500 on Lafitte's head; not to be outdone, the "Terror of the Gulf" countered with one of $1,000 on the governor's head!

By helping Andrew Jackson win the Battle of New Orleans in 1815, Lafitte's pirates turned patriots and were all granted pardons for their crimes by President Madison. Some of his group stayed in Louisiana to pursue legal enterprises, but Lafitte moved on to continue his Barataria livelihood. Sailing along the Gulf Coast, he and his new band discovered an abandoned settlement on a barrier island in 1817. Noting its natural curvature that provided pirate ships a safe harbor from which to attack, they moved right in to stay.

With his fierce reputation following him, he lorded over his colony of Campeche on Galveston's East End for three years. Befitting a pirate king, he built a grand fort and named it Maison Rouge, or the Red House, after its striking color, on the south side of what is now Harborside Drive between 14th and 15th Streets. He furnished it with the best of the booty his company captured from the slave ships. Clients, like the Bowie brothers, paid $1.00 per pound at auction for the slaves and then marched them across the Louisiana border to resell them at full market price; in two years, the Bowies made in excess of $65,000 from this enterprise, and Jean Lafitte became Galveston's first successful entrepreneur.

A tall and striking man with hazel eyes, the privateer stood at the height of his power in 1818, dispensing brutal justice as he acted as judge, jury and executioner. Nearing forty, this self-proclaimed "Lord of Galveston" traded his cocky youth for a haughty but noble bearing, returning to his highborn, blue-blooded roots and dressing the part in full military uniform when receiving guests.

One of them was the aged General Rigaud, who traveled with his much younger nurse/wife. On their way to join a French colony, Champ d'Asile on the Trinity River (near the present-day city of Liberty), they sailed into Galveston Harbor. Ever the courtly host, Jean entertained them at Maison Rouge with all the elegance of his aristocratic youth. As the firelight flickered, he stared across the room at Madame Madeline and was immediately smitten with the tall, buxom blonde—unrequited, as she left with her husband the next day.

After several months, she once again passed through Galveston—a widow this time. Madeline planned to return to France and quietly resume her nursing career. At once, Jean asked her to be his bride, but she said no, as she could not see herself as the wife of a pirate. She sailed for home aboard the *Orleans* that night at midnight.

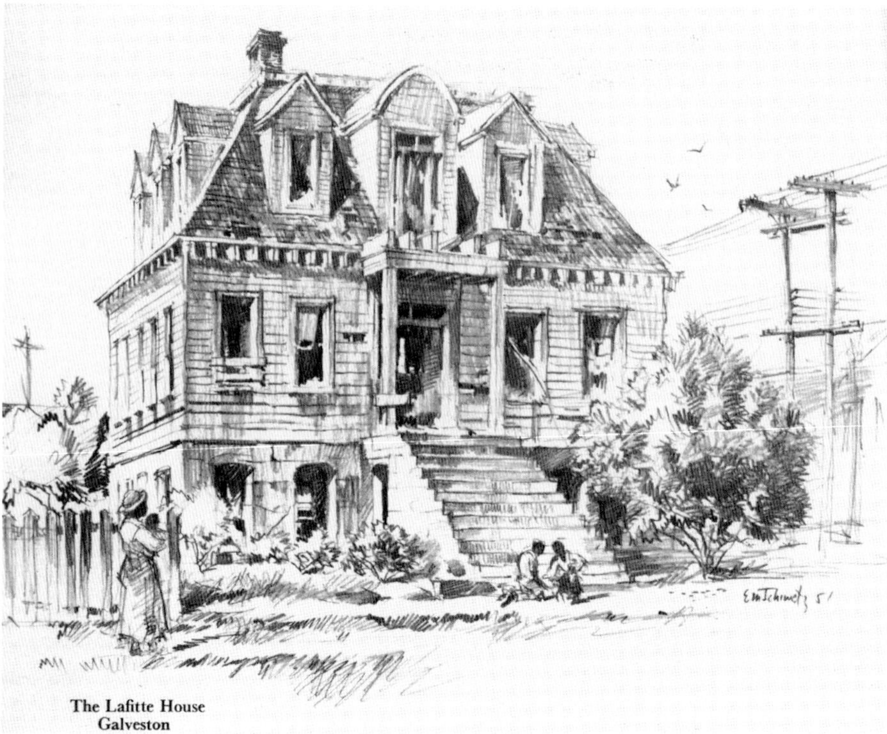

Drawing of Pirate Lafitte's Maison Rouge from *Texas Sketch Book*.

The next day, a violent hurricane hit the Island. Lafitte ordered his men to ride out the storm with him aboard his ship. In a daring move, he sailed with the wind, which brought them across the Island into the Gulf of Mexico to relative safety. After the storm had passed, they surveyed the damage and discovered the hull of a recently wrecked ship: the *Orleans*! Charging aboard in desperation, the pirate turned patriot found his Madeline lying unconscious in her half-submerged cabin. Gathering her in his arms, he rescued her from certain death.

Months after she had recovered her strength at his Red House, Lafitte once again offered marriage. This time, she seriously pondered her decision. "Who was this man: French nobleman, buccaneer…entrepreneur?" After learning of his heroics in the Battle of New Orleans from Andrew Jackson himself, Madame Madeline deemed Lafitte a hero, an officer and a true patriot. They were married in the great hall of Maison Rouge by an old French priest and lived together happily, soon expecting an heir.

Nine months later, however, she died in childbirth. It was as though the pirate's spirit died with her. Swearing that he'd buried his treasure on the West End at the site of the Three Trees, he left Galveston a broken man in 1820, burning his colony to the ground. The freebooters who stayed behind rushed to the site to recover it. They found no treasure per se, only a long box containing the body of a woman—Jean Lafitte's beloved Madeline.

PETER AMES VINCENT, REGISSEUR

Passionate about his chosen profession, Peter Ames Vincent lived a most theatrical life. Cast as the first artistic director of Galveston's Little Theatre, he connected his adopted home to the performing arts world by propelling his small Island stage into the spotlight of the national local/regional theater movement.

Upon graduation from Cornell University, he served apprenticeships in New York City, Boston and Seattle. Specializing in theatrical costume and scenic design, he was stage manager and scenic designer under the direction of Howard Mumford Jones at the University of Texas–Austin. Impressed with Vincent's talent, Dr. Jones sent his student to speak to Galveston's literary ladies about the Little Theatre's role in the future of American dramatic literature. The women of the board hired him immediately.

After the seasons ended in May, Vincent continued to study the new stagecraft on Broadway and the Continent. Attending and critiquing performances of the latest plays, he implemented the new techniques at local theaters nationwide before bringing his mastery home with him. Secure in his new role/title as Regisseur, he became a prolific writer on all subjects theatrical—in particular, the effect of theaters on their communities. Many of his articles appeared in respected journals of the theater world, such as *Billboard* and *Theatre Arts Monthly*. When he wasn't directing, studying or writing, he was lecturing on the subject.

January 1929, however, signaled the beginning of the end when Peter Ames Vincent fell ill. When he was hospitalized, his protégé, Gladys Ann Kirschner, stood in for the director, as "the shows must go on." For his part, he worked from his hospital bed until he became too ill. To ease his mind, the women of the board guaranteed payment of all his medical bills. Chosen by him in the fall of 1929, the spring production that year was most suitable: *The Circle* by Somerset Maugham.

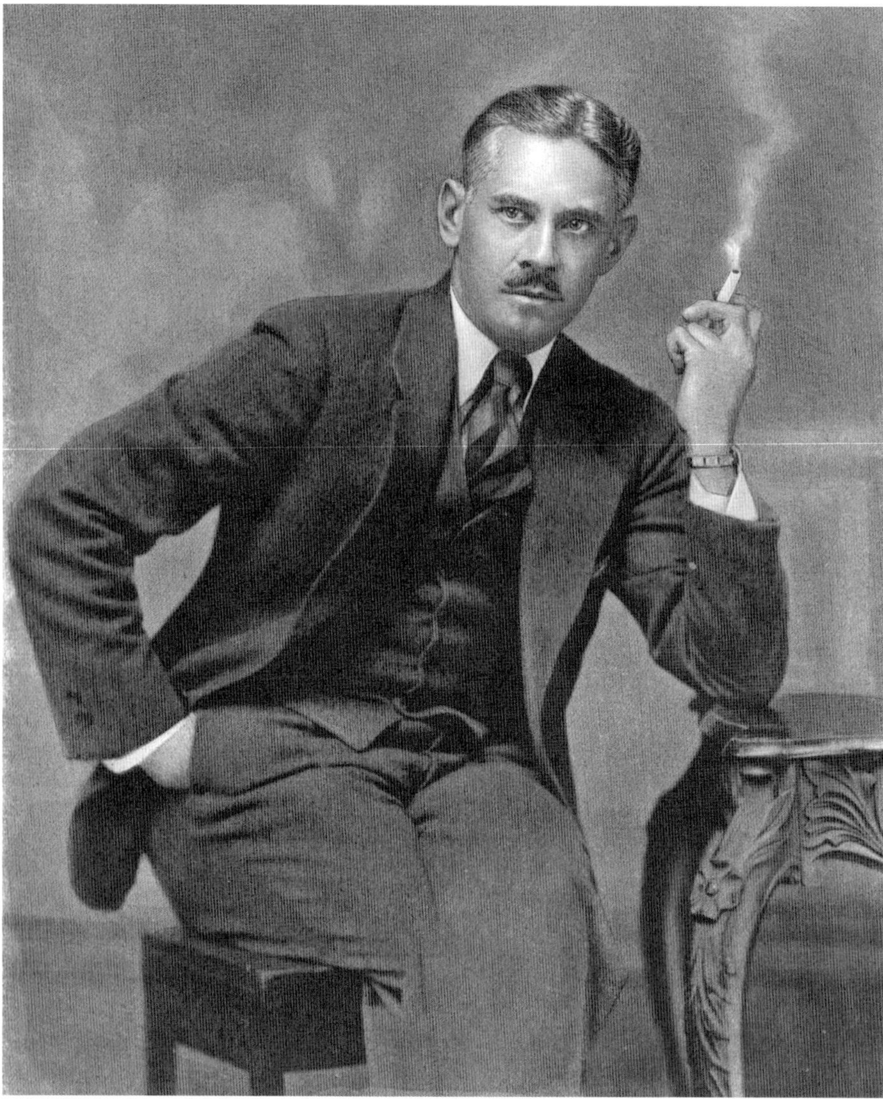

Peter Ames Vincent, Regisseur, Little Theater of Galveston. *Courtesy of the Rosenberg Library, Galveston, Texas.*

Peter Ames Vincent died shortly after noon on April 16, 1930. Born at Nyack, New York, on October 23, 1884, he died in Galveston from cancer of the bladder. His obituary in the *Tribune* stated, "Under his direction, the Little Theatre group became recognized throughout the country for their high degree of artistic excellence in productions." He was buried at Lakeview Cemetery on the Island; his simple white marble headstone, also purchased by the Little Theatre, was inscribed, "A Genius Dwelt Among Us."

Three months after his death, Vincent revealed his deep love for Galveston that had developed through his love of its theater from beyond the grave. An essay entitled "An Island Theatre" appeared in the July 1930 issue of *Theatre Arts Monthly*. Using the language of a poet, he described the strange presence of the surrounding sea that both "isolates and connects us....Perhaps, because we are islanders, we do not care for what the rest of the Little Theatre world thinks of us....What is born on our little stage lives its brief life there, and we immediately go on to something else. It is the theatre that we serve, or rather the love of the theatre...from which we draw our courage and our faith."

The editors followed it with: "Peter Ames Vincent died at Galveston.... The theatre will continue."

BONGO JOE

Innovative percussionist and legendary Texas street performer Bongo Joe was born George Coleman in Haines City, Florida, on November 28, 1923. Orphaned at an early age, he finished high school before moving in with his sister in Detroit.

Attracted to "anything you bang on," he taught himself the piano, practicing with local musicians in jam sessions. Discovering jazz, he graduated to solo performance, even doing a gig with Sammy Davis Jr. in the Motor City.

Coleman started banging drums in Houston during the early 1950s. Even though he didn't own a full drum set, he was hired as a percussionist. Necessity being the mother of invention, he fashioned one from several empty fifty-five-gallon oil drums. This created a unique "hollow" percussive sound, similar to Jamaican steel drummers (whom he'd never heard or seen).

Over the years, he perfected his jazzy/bluesy beat, fine-tuning it in street corner concerts. Experimenting with different drumming techniques, he used pickup microphones and amplifiers to magnify the drums' pulsations. A multimedia artist of sorts, he supplemented the beats with rhythmic whistling and animal sounds, writing original songs with whimsical yet perceptive lyrics about whatever came to mind.

Moving to Galveston ten years later, he painted his drums bright, psychedelic colors during those liberated '60s, when he was a familiar sight and sound on Galveston's seawall between 25th and 23rd Streets. He accepted the affectionate nickname of "Bongo Joe" from his many Island fans who regularly "fed his kitty." He seriously considered making this city his base until a new retirement home imposed a 10:00 p.m. noise curfew, "which was when things were just getting started," according to Larry Skoog and Chris Srachwitz in a 1968 live interview.

Resolutely, this nomadic percussionist played somewhere every night, rain or shine, hauling his customized drums all over the state. HemisFair '68 brought him to San Antonio, where he played near the festival site. Attracting the attention of Strachwitz's Arhoolie Records, Coleman was persuaded to make a few recordings, which were released as an album the following year with little success. After a trip to Mexico, oil drums in tow, he played piano in Acapulco before he settled in the Alamo City at the Plaza. From here, he traveled the state and beyond.

During the next decade, his gigs further broadened his reputation. The New Orleans Jazz and Heritage Festival invited him to perform nine times, one of which featured a duet with personal favorite Dizzy Gillespie, with Bongo Joe on piano. The jazz man also played for President John F. Kennedy in Fort Worth the night before he was assassinated, and Gerald Ford's presidential campaign hired Coleman to play a ten-city tour in 1976.

He debuted on television in 1991 on three episodes of *Almost Live from the Liberty Bar*, which aired on San Antonio's PBS station KLRN. Several years later, his "failed" 1969 album was re-released as *George Coleman—Bongo Joe* and caused quite a stir.

His music was viewed everything from a novelty act to the work of an inspired, disciplined musician. The innovative percussionist, however, grew to become an underground cult favorite from several cuts on his new/old album. From Texas to England, one of its songs, "Innocent Little Doggie," became a touchstone in "edgy" jazz cultures.

Unfortunately, his newfound respect through independent radio was cut short when he was diagnosed with diabetes and kidney disease, which forced him to stop performing. He died on December 19, 1999, in San Antonio.

A real musician from the inside out, Bongo Joe is now remembered as a disciplined musician, avid performer and cult figure. An innovative free spirit who chose the street instead of the stage and preferred to live off donations rather than high-playing gigs, performer George Coleman definitely had the music in him.

"WANDERER OF THE WASTE LAND": UTAH CARL BEACH

Born on January 31, 1919, on an Indian reservation in Bartlesville, Oklahoma, Carl Jared Beach grew up in Coffeyville, Kansas. This long, six-foot-six-tall Cherokee/Irish cowboy was a born troubadour, playing guitar and singing for anyone who would listen.

At age eleven, he bought his first guitar for three dollars on an installment plan. A fortuneteller at the Coffeyville county fair launched his career a year later when she suggested he strum and sing for the local radio station, KGGF. Even though it was during the Great Depression, the twelve-year-old marched right in on a Saturday morning and was on the air before noon.

While at that station, he acquired a lifelong fan. Beach received a large number of requests via postcards signed "Juanita" to play her favorite songs. While he was playing a dance in Coffeyville, a blue-eyed brunette with bedroom eyes was introduced to him. As they danced, she looked up at him and simply said, "I'm Juanita." Call it love at first sight because Carl was smitten. They married after moving to Las Vegas.

KGGF was the first of many stations that this rockabilly guitarist would play as they wandered west. During the early 1940s, he was a strolling cowboy guitarist at the Last Frontier Hotel in Vegas. Primarily, he preferred Jimmie Rogers's songs and "sentimental" tunes that suited his yodel-like baritone.

In addition to his regular radio gig, he was a guest artist on a program named *Hymns of All Churches* for the Mutual Broadcasting Network. The first song he sang was an old cowboy standard, "Utah Carl's Last Ride." Whether by accident or design, the radio announcer effectively eliminated his last name when he started calling the troubadour by the song's title character. For the next forty-three years, he was known simply as "Utah Carl." Whether he'd ever even been to that state is still anybody's guess.

When his Vegas contract ended five years later, he moved his family to Galveston Island, where he played a regular program at radio station KULF. In 1951, he introduced his theme song, "Wanderer of the Wasteland," on the show. During the evenings, he and his band, Herbie and the Boys, would play various clubs and lounges.

His television career began two years later in a twist-of-fate kind of way. Paul Taft of Houston's Duncan Coffee partnered with several others to open the city's first TV station, KGUL, on 45th Street at Video Lane, a CBS affiliate. Broadcasting in a tri-city area (Houston, Galveston and Freeport), it was the most powerful station in the state at that time.

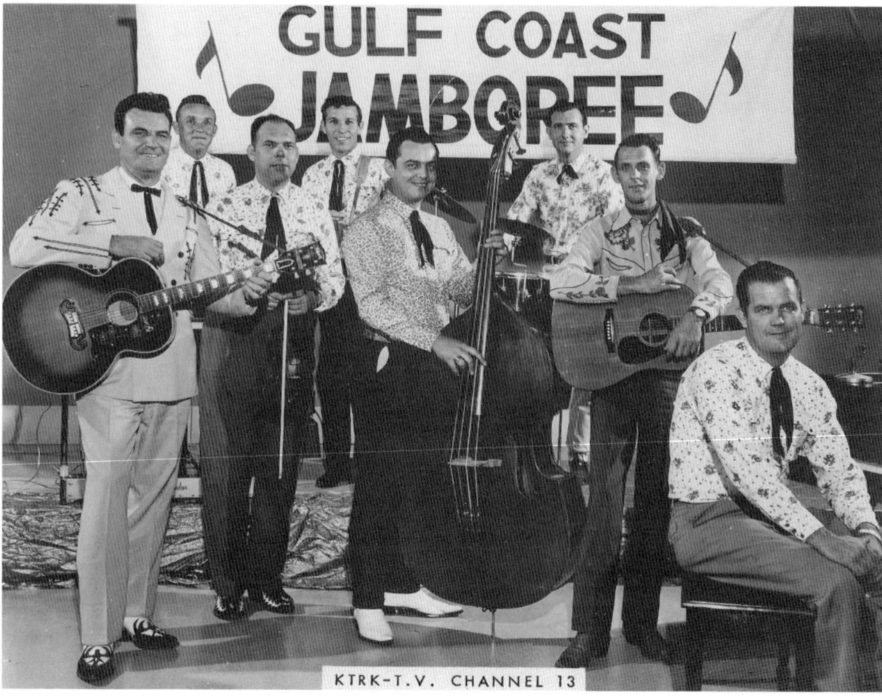

Utah Carl Beach with Herbie and the Boys. *Author's father's collection.*

One of its major investors was actor Jimmy Stewart, who came to town to host its grand opening on March 22. A Stewart movie was planned as the first program, but when the projector was switched on, nothing happened. While the actor stumblingly ad-libbed, several of Galveston's finest roused Utah Carl from sleep, rushing him to the station, where he improvised a twenty-five-minute set in the lobby. When he finished, Taft and Stewart signed him as one of the station's permanent staff members and gave him a regular time slot with his band.

This lasted fourteen years, sponsored by Gulf Coast Furniture Warehouse on Highway 35 in Alvin, which was managed by his friend, Hub Holcomb. Soon, every weekend, the singer-songwriter-entertainer could be found onstage along with his band in the warehouse's parking lot, playing old hillbilly standards, which he'd promised on their KGUL show.

During the late '50s, he recorded two of his original songs, "Daddy's Little King" and "The Man in the Moon." The release party was a western jamboree at Galveston's City Auditorium, featuring Ernest Tubb, Hank

Snow and the Texas Troubadours. He also wrote other notable tunes for Nashville's Bullet Recording Company, like "It's No, My Darling" and "Memories by My Fireside."

Although music was his passion, husband and father Carl Beach took a day job to support his family of four, who lived at 2521 Avenue Q. An insurance agent at Prudential's Galveston office, the former cowboy turned businessman proved successful at it, too, as he rose to its executive vice-president in 1966.

His forty-five-year career ended when he died on September 24, 1977. Succumbing to carcinoma of the lung at St. Mary's Hospital, Utah Carl was only fifty-seven years old. His funeral mass was set for 10:15 a.m. the following Monday morning at St. Mary's Cathedral. One of his band members borrowed instruments from Ginsberg's Music Center across the street, which Herbie and the boys set up in the church loft. Before Father Paul Chovonec began the service, the tune "Utah Carl's Last Ride" rang out over the congregation, one final tribute to the rockabilly troubadour and showman.

ROBERT DURST: INFAMOUS ISLANDER BY CHOICE

Galveston sits serenely two miles off the Texas coast in the sparkling Gulf of Mexico. Its primary entrace is literally the end of the road—Interstate 45, which, despite its name only travels from Dallas to Galveston. There, it ends at 59th Street and morphs into the city's primary west–east thoroughfare, Broadway. This completion brings many who are at the end of their ropes to lose themselves in the Island city's tree-lined streets and timeless Victorian architecture.

Rumor has it that some of these transients arrived via one-way bus tickets—a solution to the homeless problems of Texas's largest cities. In 2001, two of these social misfits—a cantankerous retired seaman and a reculsive stranger, both from New York—found themselves sharing a house with disastrous results: one lost his head to the other, who was out of his right mind.

That fall, several black garbage bags bobbed in Galveston Bay near a residential waterfront neighborhood. Upon investigation, police discovered a man's severed torso, arms and legs—but no head. An additional paper trail of evidence eventually led detectives to a blood-soaked apartment in a subdivided house on Avenue K. One of the residents, a mute bag lady named Dorothy Ciner, was home, but her neighbor, Morris Black, was not.

Sitting on one of those quiet, tree-lined streets in the center of the city's historical East End, the residence was close to the local Salvation Army, a haven for the homeless on Broadway. The public library was just around the corner, a natural neighborhood hangout for those with little to do. The odd couple could not have chosen a better place to hide in plain sight—lost among the shelves of books and periodicals.

One of the research librarians became somewhat of a confidante to Black. Finding this old cantankrous curmudgeon a sympathetic character, she listened as he shared memories of New York and confided the details of his will: he had saved more than $100,000 payable upon death to his sister, who still lived in their home state.

Little did Galveston's finest realize what they'd found near 22nd and Avenue K. The "woman" turned out to be wealthy New York heir Robert Durst, who promptly jumped the $300,000 bond he'd posted for the murder of his neighbor. Using Black's ID, the bald millionaire was discovered in Pennsylvania forty-five days later when he stole a chicken sandwich and newspaper from a grocery store. If he'd merely paid for the items with part of the $500 cash he carried, he could have gotten away scot-free; instead, he was arrested for shoplifting and extradited back to Texas.

A nationwide investigation linked Durst to two other suspected murders: the sudden disappearance of his wife, Kathleen, in New York in 1982 and the execution-style death of his friend and confidante Susan Berman in California, who was found with a bullet to the brain on the eve of her testimony into Kathy's disappearance.

Two years later, a national criminal trial, with its accompanying entourage of news media, disturbed Galveston's idyllic serenity. Bringing a dose of hard reality into this dreamy, retrospective city, litigation began on September 23, 2003, downtown at the county courthouse, just blocks away from the crime scene. A female judge whose family had a long history in the county's politics presided over the proceedings, which pitted a new district attorney against a seasoned criminal attorney, Houstonian Richard "Dick" Degurien.

Hiring the high-profile professional was the first (and maybe the only) thing Durst did right. First, his attorney pleaded self-defense and admitted to the victim's dismemberment. He then argued that based on a psychiatrist's testimony, the accused suffered from Asperger's syndrome, explaining his erratic behavior—a tactic allowed by the judge.

Deguricn then carefully crafted a scenario to plant reasonable doubt in the mind of every juror: arriving home on September 28, the accused found Black in his own apartment, waving Durst's gun around and threatening to kill him. The two men struggled, causing it to accidently discharge into his neighbor's face, killing the curmudgeon. With the defendant as the only witness, how could anyone disprove it?

To dispose of the large body, Durst walked to a local hardware store the other way on Broadway and bought a hacksaw and large black plastic garbage bags. Back at home, he systematically set about the grisly task of separating the limbs from the torso—so skillfully it prompted the judge to admit, twelve years later, that "it wasn't a first time job." Bagging the parts, he dumped them in the bay—all except the head, which would show where the bullet really landed.

On November 11, 2003, the jury delivered the unconscionable verdict of "not guilty," citing "reasonable doubt." Robert Durst was surprised—his lawyer, not so much. However, the exonerated was a free man only off and on for the next twelve years, as he kept managing to get himself jailed for other offenses, from public urination on candy to a weapons charge in New Orleans. The latter led to his extradition to California, where he was charged with the first-degree murder of friend Susan Berman in 2000; the trial, expected to start in late 2017, was postponed until April 2018, when a preliminary hearing took place. After weighing the strong evidence of guilt presented by thirteen witnesses, judgment is still pending—if Durst should live so long, as he is in very poor health and wheelchair-bound.

Finally, the end of the road will become the end of the line for this New York heir.

BOIs OFF THE ISLAND

King Vidor: Original Hollywood Producer/Director

King Wallis Vidor (pronounced "vee-*dor*") was born in Galveston on February 8, 1894, at 1702 Winnie to Charles and Katie Lee Vidor. He grew up to become one of the first successful producer/directors from the earliest days of silent movies through the Golden Age of Hollywood and beyond. In fact, Vidor is even listed in the *Guinness Book of World Records* for having the longest career as a film director, from 1913 to 1980.

His father, Charles Shelton Vidor, founded the Miller-Vidor Lumber Company in a small town in Southeast Texas, named after him (company name pronounced "*vi*-dor"). With its mills and railroads located there, its headquarters was on Galveston Island.

In 1908–9, son King attended the Peacock Military Academy in San Antonio before returning to the Island, where he started his film career as a projectionist at the Globe, the city's first movie theater. Watching the silent movies over and over again, he would study directors' cinematic techniques, or lack thereof, before experimenting with his own. While still living at home, he produced two movies—the first about his experiences during the 1900 Storm, *Hurricane in Galveston*, and the second later that year, *The Grand Military Parade*. Simultaneously, he was a newsreel photographer, filming local newsworthy events and then selling them to newsreel companies.

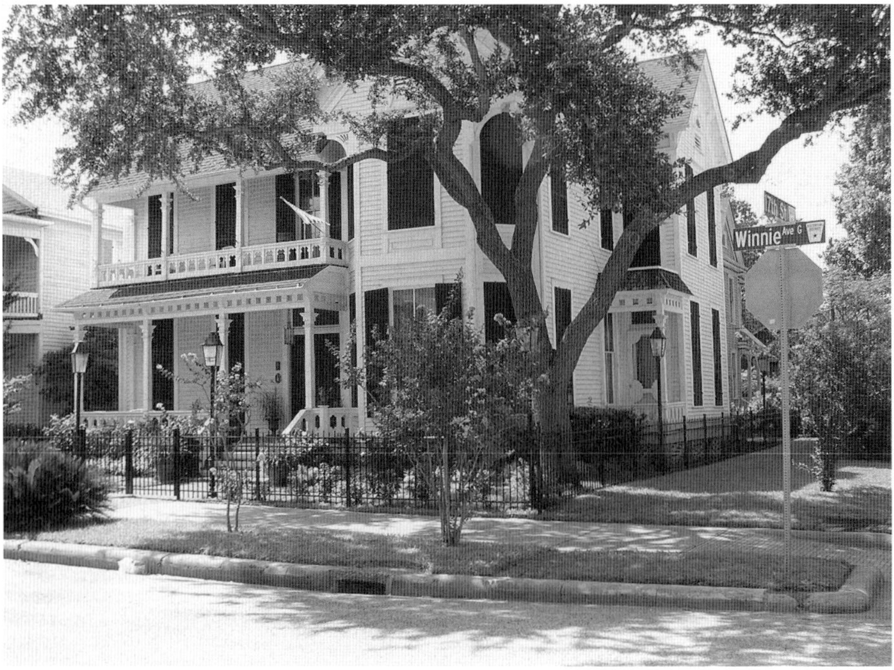

Birthplace of King Vidor, 17th and Winnie. *Author's collection.*

While at the Academy, King met Edward Sedgewick. In 1915, they moved to Houston to partner in a film studio, Hotex. Producing silent two-reelers, Vidor cast the beautiful Florence Arto in his first one and then married her. She provided the impetus for their move to Hollywood, which Vidor financed by producing an advertising newsreel for the Ford Motor Company. He started working for Universal Studios for twelve dollars a week, and before long, he was directing Mrs. Vidor, who proved the more successful of the two in the beginning.

To honor his Christian Science beliefs, he produced a movie for his church entitled *The Turn in the Road* in 1919. Throughout his career, his religious background infused his filmmaking with a sense of mission that uplifted the "everyman," exposed the horrors of war and revealed racism. The following year, he bought a square block of Santa Monica Boulevard and opened his own King Vidor Productions and acting colony, named Vidor Village.

In 1922, he went to work for Goldwyn, which was absorbed by MGM. His first breakout production was *The Big Parade* in 1925, a powerful antiwar film set during World War I staring a very young John Gilbert. Even though

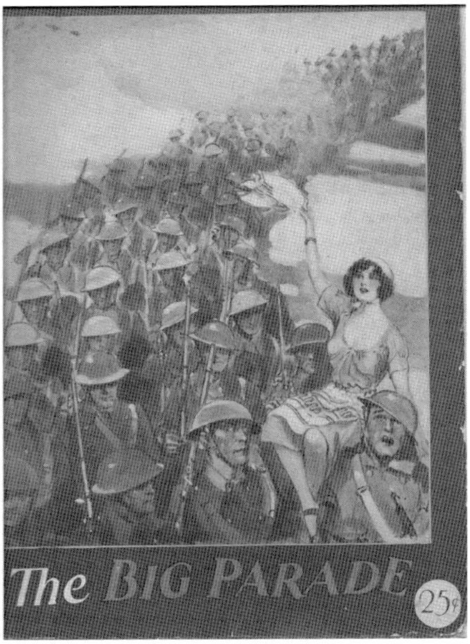

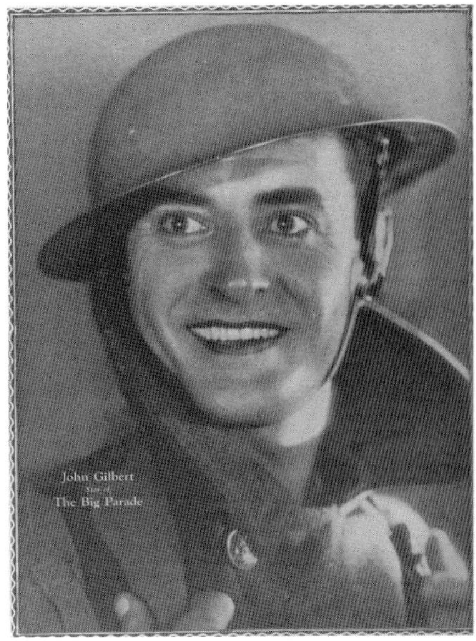

Left: Program cover sold at theaters showing the 1925 film. *Author's collection.*

Right: Star of King Vidor's antiwar movie. *Author's collection.*

Vidor's contract with the studio stipulated that the producer/director receive 20 percent of its profits, company accountants persuaded him to sell that right for a small amount, citing production costs and overruns. As it turned out, that film became MGM's most profitable to that date.

His next pioneering movie was his first sound film, 1929's *Halleluyah!* His direction of this all-black musical, expertly blending melodrama and music, earned King the first of his five Oscar nominations. Unfortunately, American culture denied him the award due to its own racial bias. In 1934, he championed the poor in his stark portrayal of the Great Depression with *Our Daily Bread*. King Vidor also directed an opera, *La Boheme*, in 1926 and *The Champ*, for which Wallace Beery won an Oscar, in 1932.

Vidor was tapped to direct the two black-and-white Kansas segments of *The Wizard of Oz* during 1938. This opportunity arose when the original director, Victor Fleming, had to replace George Cukor on David O. Selznick's high-budget epic, *Gone with the Wind*. In an interview several years before his death, he revealed that he had done this without pay or credit, as he was just trying to help out a friend. Yet his contribution to this children's classic was itself epic. Not only did it include the memorable "Somewhere Over the Rainbow" song by Judy Garland, but this sequence also presented the

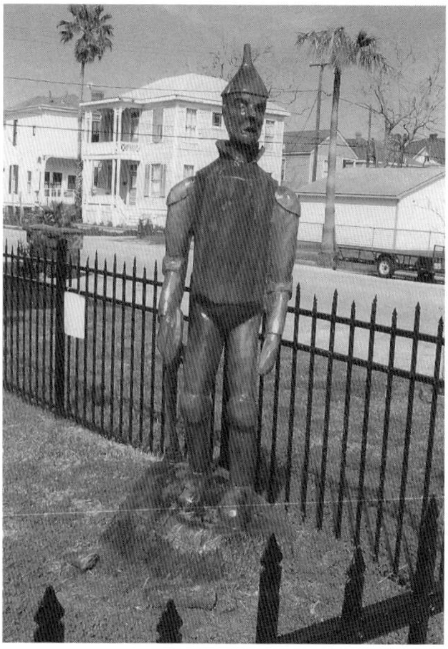

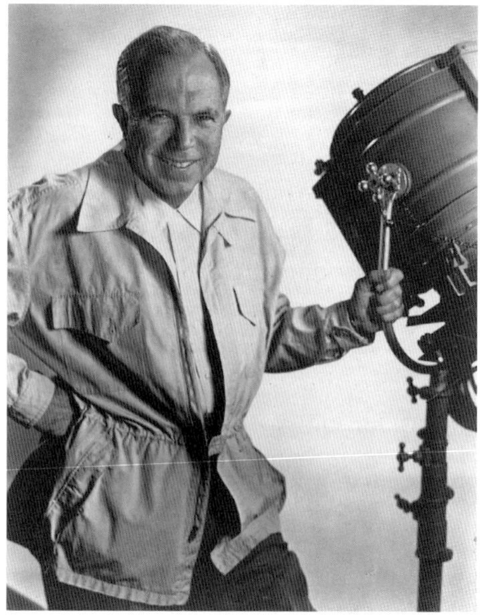

Left: Tin Woodsman tree carving in the yard of his birthplace. *Author's collection.*

Right: King Vidor, 1964. *Author's collection.*

horrifying twister sequences, which stood in sharp contrast to the colorful, unreal world of Oz.

Again for Selznick, Vidor directed the epic western *Duel in the Sun* in 1946. Although that film received many nominations, it was not a winner. Also listed among his credits are an adaptation of Ayn Rand's *The Fountainhead* in 1949 and the spectacle *War and Peace* seven years later.

Although he officially retired in 1959, Vidor taught movie craft at the University of Southern California and UCLA, both of which filmed many of his lectures for posterity. Vidor received a star in the Hollywood Walk of Fame on his sixty-sixth birthday in 1960. However, he was still 2/5 in the Oscar game until 1979, when the Motion Picture Academy presented him with an honorary award for his body of work. His final film was *Metaphor* in 1980, a documentary about his friend artist Andrew Wyeth.

Regarding his remarkable career, he once said, "My love affair with the greatest medium of expression has never faltered. It embraces all other art forms." King Wallis Vidor died at his California home on November 1, 1982, leaving a trailblazing legacy of more than fifty films in every genre.

Charlotte Walker, Broadway and Silent Screen Star and Daughter, and Sara Haden, Character Actress

During the early half of the twentieth century, this Galveston-born beauty debuted on the London stage at the age of nineteen in *The Mummy*, a farce comedy about resurrecting the ancient Egyptian pharaoh Rameses. Playing opposite company owner Richard Mansfield, she received outstanding reviews by the critics. The *Daily Mail* called her a "very promising, pretty and charming young comedienne," while the *Topical Times* lauded the American actress for her "humor, brightness and excellent appearance." A charming beauty, Charlotte was catapulted to the big time as soon as the final curtain fell—she sailed for New York City with Mansfield for the 1896–97 Broadway season.

She had discovered her flair for the dramatic early on. By age ten, she'd already attained the title "tragedienne" at the Burg Theater in Weissenbach, Germany, where she received her friends the empress of Austria and Archduchess Valarie. Born to an affluent Galvestonian who founded the cotton brokerage of Walker, Fowler and McVitie, Charlotte grew up surrounded by wealth.

Before that, she appeared onstage locally from 1886 until 1895, using the comedic recitation as her vehicle. The *Galveston Daily News* noted her performances on a regular basis in 1894—first in *Chrysanthemums* for the Trinity Guild and then in the novel entertainment *The King's Daughter* at the Cathedral Hall, where she told the tale of the "One Legged Goose," which was noted as being "overwhelming." That December, she joined Misses Lucy Hickenlooper and M. Goggan in a musical and literary show for several encores.

The following year, however, her father died, and the family moved to a ranch owned by her even wealthier mother, Charlisa de Ganahl Walker. "Miss Lotte" studied acting and drama as a teenager at the Fort Edwards Collegiate Institute; this led to an invitation to act with the Richard Mansfield Company. With her mother as chaperone, she debuted in Atlanta, Georgia, where she received critical acclaim from the *Constitution* in the chief role of Maggie in *Prince Karl* in 1896.

On the heels of her success in Georgia, her personal life interrupted her professional career when she married Dr. John B. Haden at St. Matthew's Church in New York City in November of that same year. Her first daughter, Beatrice Shelton Haden, was born in 1897 while the newlyweds were living in an apartment overlooking Central Park, the

San Remo. Moving back to Galveston to 2321 Avenue O, Katherine Haden came along two years later; also an actress, she who would became better known as Sara Haden. Both girls attended Sacred Heart Academy as a boarding school.

After her divorce from Haden in 1903, Charlotte received professional theatrical training at the Chase Art School, which again led to a five-year contract to play principal parts. She sailed back to New York on the Mallory Lines in 1906, successfully returning to the Broadway stage and reaching the pinnacle of her career.

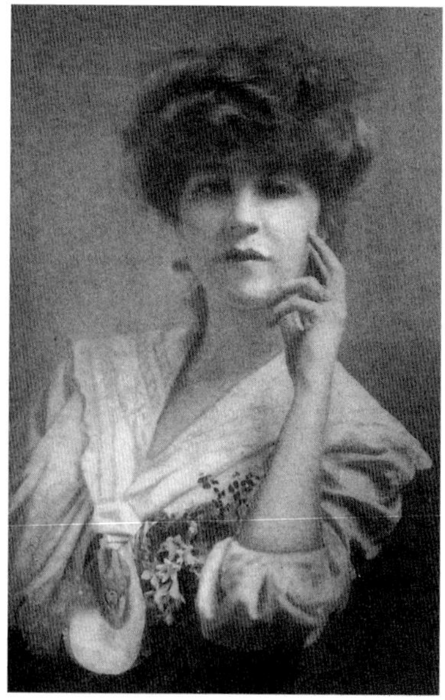

Charlotte Walker, undated. *Author's collection.*

In 1908, she married prolific playwright Eugene Walter, who adapted the novel *The Trail of the Lonesome Pine* as a vehicle for her in 1911. Within two years, she scored her biggest success. Noticing her in *On Parole*, David Belasco signed her to star in his stage productions *The Warrens of Virginia*, *Just a Wife* and *Call the Doctor* before World War I.

Miss Walker would reprise her *Lonesome Pine* performance in the role of June in 1916 when she acted in Cecil B. DeMille's film of the same name. Although this would begin her silent movie career, she returned to the stage for her most notable performance, in the Player's Club production of *The School for Scandal* with Ethel Barrymore in 1923.

Among her silent movie triumphs were *Kindling* and *Out of the Darkness*. In 1917, she was featured in a five-reeler in the episode entitled "Sloth," starring as a Dutch maid; its theme criticized luxury and offered a plea for a return to the simpler life of America's forefathers. One of her few notable film roles that still survives today is *The Midnight Girl* (1925), in which Charlotte played opposite a pre-Dracula Bela Lugosi.

On the road as Iris March in *The Green Hat* (and others), Miss Walker returned to her Island home in 1926. Of the new Little Theatre of Galveston, under the direction of Regisseur Peter Ames Vincent, she noted, "Not only is the Little Theater doing more than the legitimate theater to keep the drama alive outside of New York, but it is doing practically all." Praising the Island's theater's accomplishments, which had been brought to

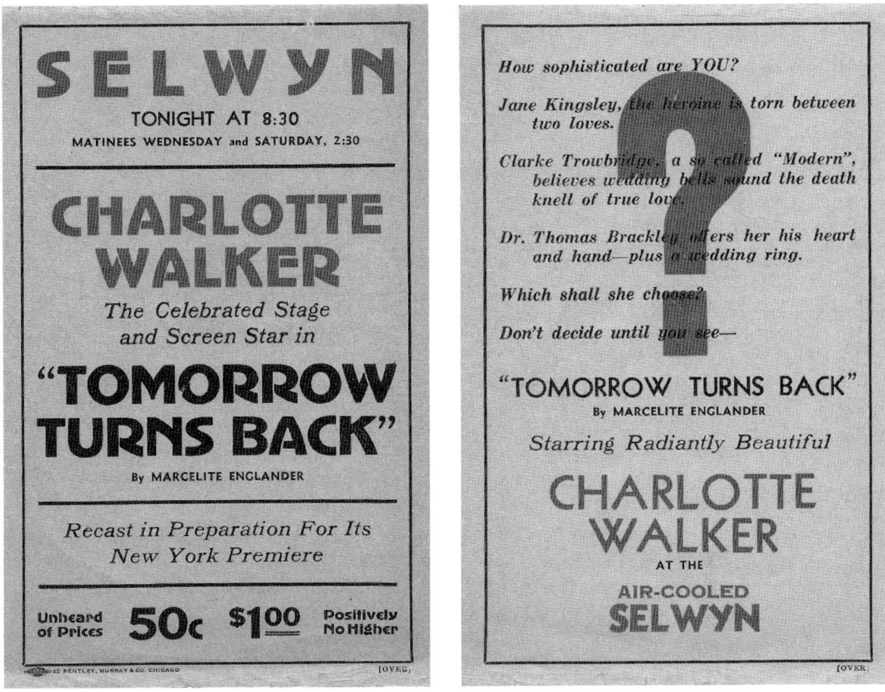

Playbill advertising Charlotte Walker in *Tomorrow Turns Back* in New York, undated.

her attention by Mrs. Richard Mansfield, she continued, "It is…up to the Little Theater to keep before the people the best type of drama and the most modern thought in the theater," as noted in various clippings from local newspapers *Galveston Daily News* and *Galveston Tribune*.

She would divorce Walter in 1930, never to marry again. Although she continued to act in films until 1941, her career seemed to decline with the beginning of the "talkies." In fact, the *New York Times* described her as "overly theatrical," a technique probably left over from her silent film/melodramatic days. She moved back to Texas and died in 1958 at age eighty-one at Kerrville hospital.

Also a BOI on November 17, 1899, her younger daughter, Sara Haden, became a character actress in film. She debuted in 1934's *Spitfire*, a vehicle for Katharine Hepburn. Lacking her mother's beauty, she was primarily typecast as the lonely school marm-type. As a contract player for MGM, she played the spinsterish Aunt Milly Forrest in the *Andy Hardy* series and also appeared in *The Shop Around the Corner* (1940) and *The Bishop's Wife* (1947). She died in California on September 15, 1981.

BOYER GONZALES SR.: FIRST NATIONALLY RECOGNIZED HISPANIC ARTIST

On September 22, 1864, Boyer Gonzales was born to socially prominent Thomas and Edith Boyer Gonzales, the fourth of five children. After one of Galveston's yellow fever epidemics claimed the lives of his two sisters, his mother fled the Island to give birth to her next baby in Houston. Although born off the Island, the privileged boy grew up here in a mansion on Avenue O and considered himself *of* Galveston.

Educated in private schools, the intelligent but introverted boy attended tea dances at the Garten Verein. He loved spending time in the West End, where he and his brothers hunted ducks. Even though he showed much natural talent as an artist early on, young Boyer was groomed to take over his family's shipping agency, Thomas Gonzales & Son, based at the Galveston port. While working at his father's successful cotton brokerage firm, he started sketching during his extended business trips.

One of his boyhood friends was Arthur Homer, who grew up to own a rope factory on the Island. In 1877, Homer introduced Boyer to his older brother, the celebrated American artist Winslow Homer. A fast friendship grew between the two painters through words and letters.

During one of his extended vacations, the young Texas artist visited his sister in Boston, with a tour of Maine's coast planned to visit with Homer at Prout's Neck, New York. As a result, their friendship grew into a mentorship as the two men spent many summers fishing and sketching together at the master's studio, which profoundly influenced Gonzales's bold watercolor style.

After a lengthy business trip in 1892 to England and the Netherlands, Boyer spent a month at a spa in Schwalbach, Germany. From here, he executed his own grand tour of Europe, drawing and painting his way across the Continent, specifically journeying to Switzerland, Italy and France. Returning to the States, he continued to concentrate on his art in Colorado before attending the World's Columbian Exposition in Chicago in 1893, brush in hand.

Months after his mother's death later that year, Gonzales traveled alone to Mexico in January 1895, specifically to paint. Ironically, the first nationally recognized Hispanic artist also became the first American painter to capture that country's lush landscape, vibrant culture and remote villages. His series of watercolors marked Boyer's movement from amateur to professional artist.

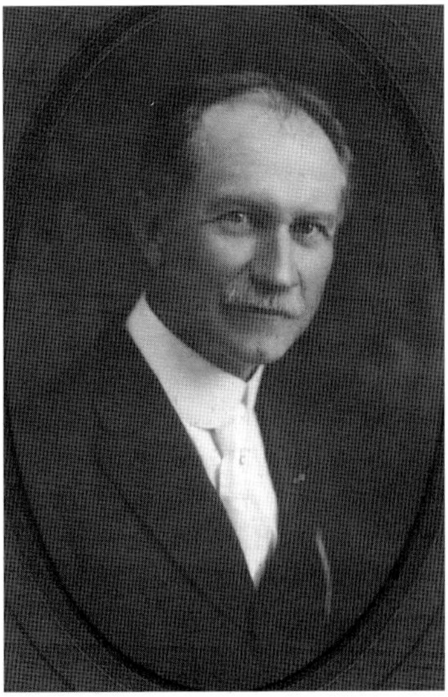

Boyer Gonzales Sr. *Courtesy of the Rosenberg Library, Galveston, Texas.*

Recognizing his need for formal training, he sought out noted York colorist William J. Wittemore, traveling later that year to Annisquam, Massachusetts, to spend three weeks working with the master. Unfortunately, however, his painting pursuit was interrupted by his father's death at the end of 1895.

The aspiring artist found himself in control of the family's business—something he did *not* want to do. Resigned to his role, he settled on Galveston Island, working as a bookkeeper for about four years, but he continued painting. In fact, he spent the summer of 1900 in Boston, where he trained with Walter Lansil, who in turn introduced him to the art of the Dutch master of maritime painting Hendrick Willem Mesdag. Boyer sold Thomas Gonzales & Sons the following year so that he could devote all of his time to painting and exhibitions. As a result, in 1904 he was invited to exhibit his works in the Texas Pavilion at the St. Louis World's Fair.

Gonzales married his longtime hometown acquaintance, Eleanor "Nell" Hertford, in New York City's Little Church Around the Corner on September 21, 1907. Winslow Homer sent the couple two of his watercolors as a wedding gift for their honeymoon home. That same day, they discovered that Boyer had been accepted to study with Birge Harrison at the Art Students League of New York in Woodstock, which was a popular artists' colony. He would also paint in Taos, New Mexico, and Monhegan Island, Maine, and occasionally returned to Mexico.

To celebrate his success, Mr. and Mrs. Gonzales left on an extended trip to Europe that would include a face-to-face meeting with Mesdag, whose marine scenes would influence Boyer's later paintings. After visiting England, Germany and Switzerland, the couple settled in Florence, where he studied with several respected Italian painters.

Painted both in oil and watercolors, his subjects varied with his locations, but he was best known for his coastal scenes of Texas and Maine. He won praise for his representations of marine life, as well as his detailed knowledge of ship construction, winning medals in Dallas in both 1921 and 1924. He also won a prize at the Southern States Art League exhibition in Fort Worth in 1926. His paintings have been exhibited at Houston's Museum of Fine Arts, as well as galleries at Dallas, Waco and the Salmagundi Club in New York City.

Boyer Gonzales Sr. died on February 14, 1934, in New York while completing a biographical sketch on Winslow Homer. The Witte Museum in San Antonio mounted solo exhibits of his work in both 1927 and 1936; the latter was circulated to other Texas museums as a memorial to the artist.

Galveston's Rosenberg Library now owns more than two hundred of his paintings, including his best-known work, *The Dawn of Texas*, depicting Sieur de La Salle's ship anchored in Matagorda Bay. Also included in the library's collection is one Winslow Homer watercolor, *Woman on a Beach*, gifted to the newlyweds on October 4, 1907.

BOYER GONZALES JR.

In early 1909, the Gonzaleses returned home to Galveston to welcome the birth of their only child on February 11. While he would spend his formative years on the Island, Boyer Jr. mainly remembered the home and studio in Woodstock, New York. His father built it ten years later to spend the summers there, with winters spent in San Antonio and Galveston. This was the environment in which they raised their son, surrounded by art and artists.

Graduating with a BS in architecture from the University of Virginia in 1931, Junior soon turned his attention to painting, primarily studying under abstractionist Henry Lee McFee at Woodstock. Based on his studies of Paul Cézanne's landscape abstracts, he turned to abstractions of natural forms as his medium. His artistic talent was recognized in 1935, when he was invited to participate in the Fourteenth Biennial Exhibition of Contemporary American Oil Paintings at the Corcoran Gallery in Washington. This led to other group shows in New York and Pennsylvania, as well as the Texas Centennial at the Dallas Museum of Art.

Moving to San Antonio in 1937, Gonzales, along with his mentor, McFee, opened the Museum School of Art via the Witte Museum, which began his art instruction career. Two years later, he accepted a faculty position at the University of Texas–Austin while still pursuing exhibitions nationwide, thus building a national reputation. His first solo exhibits were in Texas, at the Witte and the Museum of Fine Arts, Houston.

From 1942 to 1946, World War II halted Boyer's art career as he served in the United States Army Air Corps, as well as in the Philippines and Japan. Upon his discharge, he married Elizabeth Cullyford Bole on December 28, 1946, and returned to UT–Austin; this eventually led to his directorship of the art school at the University of Washington–Seattle, a position he held from 1954 to 1966.

Over the years, the younger Boyer Gonzales's style developed from realism to bold abstractions in the colors of nature, using oils on canvas, panel and ink, pencil or conté crayon on paper. He defined a successful piece of art as one with "an inner spirit and life of its own." At the end of his life on July 27, 1987, he had shown in more than forty group exhibitions, with thirteen solo shows. Many of his works remain part of the permanent collections at San Antonio's Witte Museum, as well as at sites in Dallas, Seattle and Tacoma.

BIBLIOGRAPHY

Beasley, Ellen, and Stephen Fox. *Galveston Architecture Guidebook.* Houston: Rice University Press, 1996.

Cartwright, Gary. *Galveston: A History of the Island.* New York: Atheneum, Macmillan Publishing Company, 1991.

Cherry, Bill. "How Sam, Rose and Frank Maceo Created the Fabled Balinese Room." *Galveston County Daily News*, July 13, 2003.

Davis, Brian M. *Images of America: Lost Galveston.* Charleston, SC: Arcadia Publishing, 2010.

Eisenhour, Virginia. *Galveston: A Different Place.* N.p.: self-published, 1986.

Ferber, Edna. *A Kind of Magic.* Garden City, NY: Doubleday & Company Inc., 1963.

Fields, F.T. *Texas Sketchbook.* Illustrated by E.M. Schiwetz. Houston, TX: Humble Oil and Refining Company, 1956.

Finstuen, Doc. "Naughty Galveston: Sin City of the Southwest." *Gaming Times*, "You Bet Your Life" column (June 1997–January 1998).

"Galveston: All America City Awards Presentation Banquet." Program, May 16, 1962. Galveston-Texas History Center, Rosenberg Library, Galveston, Texas.

Galveston Daily News. Various articles, 1841–2012.

Galveston Historic Homes Tour Brochures. Galveston Historical Foundation, 1974–2012.

Galveston Tribune. "Brought Chicle to Galveston in 1869: How Treasure Island Missed Being Chewing Gum Capital of World." September 11, 1925.

———. "Passing of a Pioneer." May 7, 1928.

Henson, Margaret Swett. "Founding the Galveston City Company: Nineteenth-Century Politics." *Galveston Chronicles: The Queen City of the Gulf.* Edited by Donald Willett. Charleston, SC: The History Press, 2013.

———. *Samuel May Williams: Early Texas Entrepreneur.* College Station: Texas A&M University Press, 1976.

Holly, Joe. "Historian Takes Aim at State Navy's Forgotten Role in Texas Revolution." *Houston Chronicle*, September 10, 2016.

Hotel Galvez: Queen of the Gulf. Galveston, TX: Mitchell Historic Properties, 2010.

Hyman, Harold M. *Oleander Odyssey: The Kempners of Galveston, Texas, 1854–1980s.* College Station: Texas A&M University Press, 1990.

Internet Movie Database. "Charlotte Walker." https://www.imdb.com/name/nm0907608.

———. "Katherine Helmond." https://www.imdb.com/name/nm0001340/?ref_=fn_al_nm_1.

———. "Sara Haden." https://www.imdb.com/name/nm0352774/?ref_=fn_al_nm_1.

Jean Lafitte, Gulf Coast Pirate and Privateer. jeanlafitte.net.

Joe, Bongo. Interview by Larry Skoog and Chris Strachwitz, San Antonio, Texas, 1968.

Kempner, Isaac Herbert. "The Galveston Commission Form of Government." Address delivered on February 12, 1946, before the Galveston Historical Society.

Little Theatre of Galveston Papers. Galveston-Texas History Center, Rosenberg Library, Galveston, Texas.

Look. "All America Cities: Galveston, TX" (April 10, 1962). Galveston-Texas History Center, Rosenberg Library, Galveston, Texas.

Machann, Clinton, and James W. Mendl. *Krasna Amerika: A Study of the Texas Czechs, 1851–1939.* Austin, TX: Eakin Press, 1983.

McComb, David G. *Galveston: A History.* Austin: University of Texas Press, 1986.

Michel Branamour Menard Vertical File. Galveston-Texas History Center, Rosenberg Library, Galveston Texas.

Pinckard, Jane Burton, and Rebecca Sealy Pinckard. *Lest We Forget: The Open Gates.* Houston, TX: self-published, 1988.

Remmers, Mary W. *Going Down the Line: Galveston's Red-Light District Remembered.* N.p.: self-published, 1997.

Reymershoffer Family Papers, 1897–1931. No. 96-0013, Galveston-Texas History Center, Rosenberg Library, Galveston, Texas.

Reymershoffer Photo File, Oversize. Galveston-Texas History Center, Rosenberg Library, Galveston, Texas.

A Riding and Walking Tour of a Residential Community Listed in the National Register of Historic Places. Galveston, TX: East End Historical District Association. Various revisions, dates.

Rosenberg Library. Galveston and Texas History Center, Galveston, Texas. Additional archival materials.

———. Newspaper archives, various subjects. http://rosenberg-library.org.

Rosenberg Library Museum Book Club. "With Bold Strokes," with special guest Ed Simmen. Program, February 15, 2014.

Ruff, Ann. "Financier of the Revolution: Samuel May Williams, Galveston, 1836." *Unsung Heroes of Texas*, n.d.

Sacred Places: Galveston's Historic Religious Institutions Tour Brochures, vols. 2, 6, 7, 14th annual. Galveston Historical Foundation.

Scardino, Barrie, and Drexel Turner. *Clayton's Galveston.* College Station: Texas A&M University Press, 2000.

Scarlett, Harold. "Back to the Balinese." *Houston Post*, December 16, 1990.

Tempo. "Galveston's Gaudy Years" (August 3, 1969).

Texas Historical Commission Atlas Online. Austin, Texas Historical Commission. http://atlas.thc.state.tx.us.

Texas Sketch Book. N.p., 1960s. Featuring sketch of Lafitte's house sketch.

Texas Star Flour Mill File of Historical Mounts. Galveston-Texas History Center, Rosenberg Library, Galveston, Texas.

Texas Star Flour Mill Records. No. 83-0045, Galveston-Texas History Center, Rosenberg Library, Galveston, Texas.

Texas State History Association. The Handbook of Texas Online. https://tshaonline.org/handbook.

Thomas Goggan and Brothers Inc. Vertical and Ephemera Files. Galveston-Texas History Center, Rosenberg Library, Galveston, Texas.

Wiencek, Henry. *The Moodys of Galveston and Their Mansion*. Galveston, TX: Mary Moody Northen Endowment, 2010.

INDEX

D

E

F

G

H

M

N

O

S

T

ABOUT THE AUTHOR

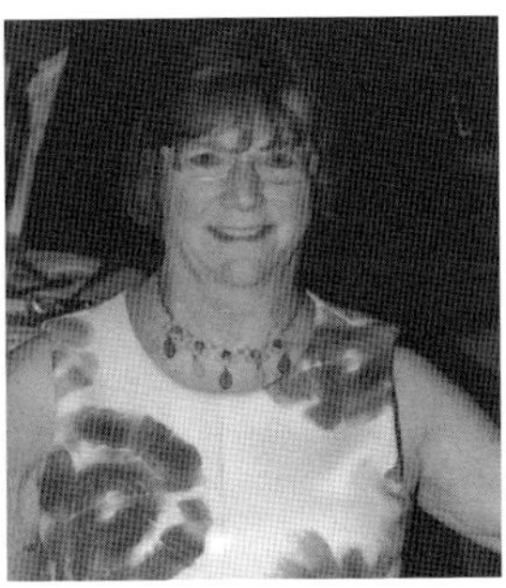

A fifth-generation "BOI," Jan Marie Johnson has been seriously studying Galveston's rich history since 1982, when she became a step-on tour guide. Originally trained through the Galveston Historical Foundation, she went beyond its notes, intentionally making it her business to learn as much of the city's past as possible.

Her interest in the Island's history began when her mother, Dorris Stechmann Johnson, became secretary to John Garner, a preservation/architect. In July 1966, this Texas-born "authority on nineteenth-century architecture" conducted a block-by-block investigation of the possibility of historical preservation in the city. His initial Historic American Buildings Survey concluded that viable and valuable historic structures existed in every area, which put the Island city at the forefront of the preservation movement. Garner also recommended that knowledgeable tour guides be trained to lead tours of the historic areas, telling visitors about Galveston's glorious history.

Jan earned a Bachelor of Science degree in elementary education at the University of Houston–Clear Lake in 1986, with a GPA of 3.94. Disenchanted with the public school system, she started her quest for a Master of Literature degree (with the intention of writing) and graduated from the same college in 1995. Taking the "freefall with free-lancing," she opened her one-person micro-business five years later: Galveston Island Gal—Writer, Tour Guide, Teacher.

At the suggestion of friends Sally and Jim Laney, she wrote her first book, *Walking Historic Galveston: A Guide to Its Neighborhoods*, fourteen years later. The first comprehensive guidebook of the Island, it focused on the city's structures built after the 1839 founding of the city in the most concentrated and recognized districts. It was published in April 2009, after the devastation of Hurricane Ike on September 13 of the previous year. She hopes to update the walking guide in the future.

With so many subjects left over, Jan was encouraged to begin *Beyond the Beaten Paths: Driving Historic Galveston*. Published in December 2012, her second book focused on those historic buildings that were scattered throughout the Island, literally "few and far between." In addition, it included brief biographies of a few of the city's most notable residents. At the request of several friends, this guide also featured an explanation of the various distinctive plaques and historical markers found on houses or in front yards throughout the city.

Unforgettable Galveston Characters is a natural progression from the places to the people of the Island. In particular, Jan was most pleasantly surprised to find so many BOIs from the professional world of entertainment, including actress Charlotte Walker and her daughter, Sara Haden; international concert pianist Olga Samaroff; and Hollywood producer/director King Vidor, as just a few examples found in this third book.